The History of the

MELTON MOWBRAY PORK PIE

A selection of traditional Melton Mowbray pork pies.

A woodcut of a Hampshire sow by Rigby Graham. This form of illustration is the earliest method of decorative printing, practised by the Chinese many centuries before the development of printing with movable type in Europe, in the 1450s: an appropriate leading illustration in a book involving pigs. The pig was domesticated around six thousand years ago, also in China.

THE BEST OF BRITISH *in Old Photographs*

The History of the
MELTON
MOWBRAY
PORK PIE

TREVOR HICKMAN

SUTTON PUBLISHING LIMITED

First published in 1997 by
Sutton Publishing Limited
Phoenix Mill · Thrupp · Stroud
Gloucestershire · GL5 2BU

**British Library Cataloguing in Publication
Data**
A catalogue record for this book is available from
the British Library.

ISBN 0-7509-1627-3

Front cover: Production of Melton Mowbray pork
pies in the 1890s.
Back cover: Production of Melton Mowbray pork
pies in the 1990s.

By the same author:
Around Melton Mowbray in Old Photographs
Melton Mowbray in Old Photographs
The Vale of Belvoir in Old Photographs
The History of Stilton Cheese
Around Rutland in Old Photographs
East of Leicester in Old Photographs
The Melton Mowbray Album

Typeset in 10/12 Perpetua.
Typesetting and origination by
Sutton Publishing Limited.
Printed in Great Britain by
Ebenezer Baylis, Worcester.

Pigs in pleasant surroundings, foraging along the banks of a river, 1924.

CONTENTS

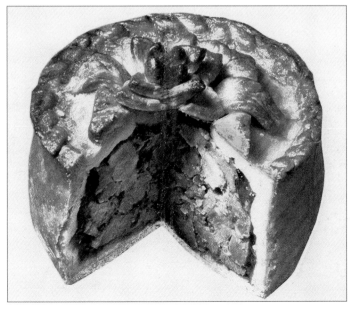

A decorated hand-raised Melton Mowbray pork pie, a pie that could be served at any huntsman's breakfast table.

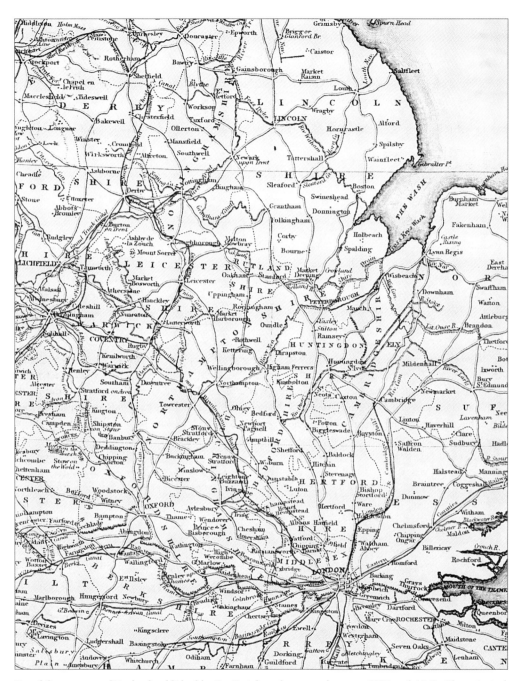

Detail from a map of England published by R. Creighton between the years 1831 and 1842. The principal stagecoach routes and the major railway lines are shown. These were being laid at that time and eventually dominated the transport system of the late nineteenth century and most of the first half of the twentieth. These transport systems connected Melton Mowbray with London and other cities, and were the reason that the pork pie made at Melton Mowbray was eaten nationally and, eventually, internationally.

INTRODUCTION

The name Melton Mowbray is synonymous with pork pies. Travel to most countries in the western world, mention this famous market town and the comment is more often than not 'the home of the Melton Mowbray Pork Pie', followed by 'of course it is also famous as a centre for Stilton Cheese and a venue for fox hunters'. Fox hunting and Stilton cheese production are two of the reasons why the famous hand-raised pork pie developed in this area. In the first section of this book I outline the history and development of the pie and in the following sections I describe its production.

One of my earliest memories is the making of hand-raised pork pies in my home on a smallholding in the village of Wymondham near Melton Mowbray in the late 1930s. Like so many smallholders and cottagers my parents raised a pig for Christmas, and because we had a larger area of land than many of our neighbours we raised two pigs, one for the home and one to sell.

My father belonged to the 'pig club'. This was a group of pig owners who formed a club to protect their annual pig slaughter. A fat pig 'well hung' was essential in maintaining sustenance in a village community throughout the year. The slaughter was a seasonal ritual, carefully controlled during the autumn months to allow offerings from each household to be circulated to all interested parties: these were the pig owners and the providers of the weekly 'swill'. The club also protected the value of the pig during its short life. If it succumbed to disease or died prematurely payment was made to the owner out of the fund – a form of insurance. Dues to the club were collected weekly at the local public house, and all surplus cash was paid out as a dividend to the members at the end of the 'season'.

One of my duties as a small child was to collect the buckets of waste vegetable products from various cottagers in the village who did not raise a pig. The contents of the bucket were placed in a large iron copper over an open fire, strategically placed in the open near the pig sty. Into this copper were placed all sorts of vegetable waste and other leftovers from meals from the dinner table, along with 'pig potatoes', small potatoes considered too small for use in the kitchen, that were separated from the main crop when they were dug up in the cottage vegetable garden. Specially bought-in meal, a form of very crudely ground flour substance obtained mainly from unwanted wheat wholemeal, and finally water were added. As the mixture boiled it was well mashed, eventually being fed to the ravenous pig, so this farm-yard animal developed into a very fat porker that was slaughtered in the autumn, a gruesome weekend process. Selected portions of the pig were made up into 'fries' and distributed to family, friends and other interested parties, normally on a Monday morning. Sufficient meat and offal was 'plated' so that it would last the recipients' households through the week. It was considered bad luck to wash the plate – it was returned to the provider with all the dried blood intact. A rotation of killing was observed, which meant there was a community distribution system to all the households involved.

Most of the pig was salted down as sides of bacon or hams. Lard was made from the soft fat linings of the carcass: this produced scrumptious pork 'scratchings' (the leftovers after the rendering process). Brawn was made from the head, 'chitterlings' from the intestines and choice portions of pork were made into pork pies.

My mother made excellent pork pies (as did most housewives living in village communities in this area of England) using hot water pastry made with fresh lard obtained from the freshly killed pig. The pastry

Elsie May Hickman, the author's mother, 1939. Elsie made excellent pork pies every autumn and winter for most of her married life from pork obtained from pigs that were fattened on her husband's smallholding. Two pigs were normally raised, one to be slaughtered in early autumn, the other just before Christmas, so that the traditional Christmas breakfast pork pie could be made a few days before the festivities began.

was moulded to form a case around a 2lb glass jam jar that was heated with warm water. The pastry case was filled with selected pieces of pork cut very small and well mixed with dried herbs that had been prepared during the summer months, to my mother's own recipe, and a cover of pastry was attached to the top of the pastry case by moistening the edge with water, sealed with her fingers, and the surplus pastry cut away with a pair of scissors. A hole was pierced in the top of the pie, after which it was baked in a hot oven on the kitchen range. After it had cooled, liquid jelly was poured into the pie through the hole in the lid. This was a gelatine obtained by boiling clippings of skin and pieces of bone in water. In section five of this book I have included a selection of recipes for making pork pies.

Served with a little English mustard the pies my mother made were unbeatable. On Christmas day morning throughout my childhood, mother's pork pie was served with a glass of an alcoholic beverage. For over thirty years I have maintained that tradition; the difference is that we now serve a commercially made Melton Mowbray pork pie to our family and friends along with a glass of fine malt whisky.

I have unforgettable childhood memories of my mother making pork pies and my involvement in moulding the pastry to make the cases, and of producing home-made pork sausages using skins obtained by stripping out membrane from lengths of the small intestine, placing the seasoned pork mixture into a hand-turned mincing machine, filling the skins, twisting and tying each link in turn, an experience that is not forgotten – but, above all, eating the home-made product is a memory that will stay with me forever.

Today we can still eat excellent pork pies made to individual recipes. There is a world-famous pork pie manufacturer still producing excellent pies in the centre of Melton Mowbray and in adjacent villages and towns pork pies are still produced by butchers and bakers with their own unique recipes, just as my mother used to make. In the following pages I have attempted to place on record an account of a truly English product made in the heart of England for generations. It is as good as it has ever been: 'the proof of the pie is in the eating'. I trust too that the proof of my researches are evident in the reading.

Not only is this book an account of the Melton Mowbray pork pie, it is also a photographic record of a unique area of local history and I trust it will give enjoyment to many. It is my compilation and collection, made possible through the help of a number of very generous people.

Trevor Hickman
June 1997

A HISTORICAL SURVEY

To state that the manufacture of pork pies originated in Melton Mowbray would be most misleading. It is not possible to say where the first pork pie was made, almost certainly not in England! Flour to make the pastry case is the key, and the ancient Greeks were conversant with bread making and the production of pastry. Undoubtedly the first farmers, our neolithic ancestors, ground corn into flour and could have made the first crude meat pastries as early as 4000 BC in Europe. Pigs have been farmed domestically in China from 7000 BC and the practice spread throughout the world as a valuable source of easily farmed meat. Pigs will eat anything edible, vegetable or animal matter, dead or alive! They will forage for nuts, roots, carrion, worms and will eat any bird or animal that is stupid enough to get near their powerful jaws. When the author was a child, his father raised pigs on their smallholding, occasionally retaining a sow for breeding, along with other farm animals and poultry. One particular sow raised a number of litters of piglets and became a family pet, and liked nothing better than to have her head scratched by all and sundry. She always greeted her food with appreciative grunts, which attracted the attention of the resident Rhode Island Red cockerel which loved the small well-cooked 'pig potatoes'. Stealing potatoes, he settled on the pig sty wall crowing his delight. One Sunday morning while the author was feeding his friend Sally the sow, the old slow pig struck as fast as a snake. Her head turned, the proud cockerel had got too close and he was gone, in a flash, without a squawk, feathers and all. Sally had a satisfied grin on her face; her tormentor was complementing her breakfast.

Because pigs are so versatile in their feeding habits they are particularly easy to raise, but because of mistreatment by humans, they are considered by many races to be unclean. This of course is untrue. A pig living free range in a forest or on heathland is as clean as any animal. They do not lie in their own faeces by choice, only if they are mistreated by humans. This so-called uncleanliness was why the labouring class were allowed to raise pigs, and because of their omnivorous eating habits they could survive on household waste and have been mistreated for thousands of years. Thomas Bewick's 'The Netty', the wood engraving on p. 13, sums this up perfectly. Bewick was a countryman, aware of human failings. The human is defecating in the sty, the pig walking away in disgust. Which is the animal?

How did the first pork pie arrive in England? Certainly the neolithic farmers raised pigs, as did the numerous pre-Conquest Celtic tribes. Their Roman conquerors enjoyed good pork dishes and drew up detailed laws to regulate pork butchers. With the exodus of the Roman occupiers Britain was infiltrated by Saxon, Viking and Danish farmers; these Scandinavian settlers were excellent cooks conversant with the use of herbs and making stews, among other dishes. They also covered meat with pastry before baking in fire pits. After 1066 the country came under the domination of Normans who introduced what we would today term 'continental cooking'. The village peasant raised pigs simply because the animal survived by eating unwanted waste food. If the turnips went rotten or the bean crop failed the foliage and rotten roots would be devoured with gusto by the resident cottage pig which would grow large and fat during the spring and summer months. With most of the farmyard animals they were slaughtered during the autumn and early winter. Until agricultural methods changed in the late eighteenth century only breeding stock was retained. With the forming of enclosed fields and the introduction of winter feeding techniques for cattle, sheep and pigs so large stocks of animals were allowed to survive the winter, fed on turnips and hay. The alternative to putting live animals into store was to slaughter, the meat being salted down, smoked or pickled.

The autumn was the time for an abundance of pies in the peasant's cottage and the squire's farm-house. The standard pies of the East Midlands were pork pies, veal pies and veal and pork pies. Veal, like pork, was a meat product that was readily available for most of the year, obtained through killing unwanted bull calves soon after birth. The neutered bull could be kept as a beast of burden, the farm ox, but the majority of bull calves were quickly slaughtered. Until the enclosure awards took effect there was no means of raising herds of fat store beasts for meat production. A cow was raised to produce milk, calves and meat. All this was to change in the 1790s. Alongside the cottage cow would be raised the cottage pig, a versatile animal that would produce litters of piglets throughout the year to be slaughtered as required. Pork, veal and mutton were easily available meats on the Norman nobleman's table during the medieval period. Pigs in the main were the only meat supply for the peasant class, who spent their short lives in total drudgery, working their strips of land to keep their families alive. Meat was essential but would be a very rare commodity in most cottages. When the family pig was slaughtered, the whole community would be involved – see the engraving on p. 15 of a seventeenth-century village scene. The meat would have been cured and placed in store. For a short time, the peasant's family and friends would have full stomachs; the offal and internal organs would be eaten with relish, and 'paties' and 'pyes' would be made. Before the 4th Earl of Sandwich (1718–92) placed slices of cold beef between two slices of bread sometime in the middle of the eighteenth century the only method of carrying meat into the fields or on a journey was to wrap it cold in a cloth or to wrap it in pastry, cook it and then eat it cold.

Meat was probably first cooked in a pastry case in England during the early medieval period. A parcel was made up with rough pastry which was wrapped around the meat, the package was cooked, and when cool the pastry case was discarded. Written evidence is scanty and certainly any comment on the use of pork by the peasantry is virtually impossible to find. Recipes and cooking methods were passed down from generation to generation by word of mouth as only the clergy, monks and a very few noblemen were capable of writing anything down. Because the pig was considered unclean even in the small number of manuscript work books that have survived from the period little or no reference is made to the use of pork. In the Harleian collection of medieval manuscripts housed in the British Library a number of recipes have been collected; in one which was written sometime around the year 1450, it is recorded that it was possible to make a 'Pyez de Parez'. Obviously written by a Norman scribe, one line reads 'Take and smyte fayre butty of Porke'. On analysis it is possible to deduce from the recipes recorded that a pie was made by rolling out some pastry, cutting it into a circle, placing in the middle of the pastry small amounts of cut up pork, into which had been mixed some dried herbs, then folding up the pastry to form a purse either by nipping the edges together, so sealing the pastry, or drawing the pastry upwards as a parcel. It is recorded that a jelly could be made by boiling bones, so it is not beyond the bounds of possibility that a hole was left in the seal of the drawn-up parcel allowing gravy to be poured into the pie to fill out the case. This was essential, for these small pies that today we would call pasties were the forerunner of the modern sandwich. A pie carried in a pouch, pocket or retained in a piece of cloth would handle and travel more conveniently if it was a solid construction, made up of hard crust pastry well filled with meat and firm gelatine.

This is the pie of the common man, not the pie of the nobleman, and it is from this peasant's pie that the Melton Mowbray pork pie developed. That pies were served in noblemen's houses is a well-recorded fact. Their contents varied: game, poultry and all varieties of meat, especially veal and beef, were used. Pork is hardly mentioned and when it is more often than not it is in conjunction with veal. Pork was normally served at the nobleman's table as a roasted suckling pig, so-called decorated boar's head or ribs of pork. One of England's greatest gourmets was Henry VIII (1491–1547), crowned in 1509. His

A Thomas Bewick wood engraving of a Chinese pig, c. 1790. It was from this breed that all domesticated pigs were eventually bred.

Illustration from Queen Mary's Psalter, compiled in England in 1310. It depicted medieval peasants knocking down acorns for their pigs, which bear a close resemblance to the Bewick pig above.

Harvesting wheat in the 1790s, a wood engraving by Bewick. It shows a village peasant cutting the ripened standing corn with a sickle, a hard, laborious job. The wheat would then be stacked in stooks, stored in a stack and thrashed. Finally the seed would be ground into flour at the village mill or in an outhouse, using a quern or a horse-propelled mill.

banquets are legendary; his guests were expected to be seated for over seven hours being served courses of food with a sample of every type of dish available in England on offer. 'Beefs, veals and hogges' were served by the entourage of servants; pork in the main was the meat of the lower and serving class.

If contemporary recipes involving pork are scanty, illustrative material is even more elusive. From documentation that does exist it would seem that the pork pastie or pie, a familiar snack today, originated in England sometime during the fifteenth century. If one looks at the children's nursery rhyme 'Simple Simon met a pieman' some indication of the spread of small meat pies through Britain can be obtained. Reference was made in 1665 to the fact that it was a traditional verse, and where contemporary illustration to the nursery rhyme exists it is interesting to note the type of pie on offer. Early prints of about 1820 show cold meat pies being carried in a wicker basket. The Catnach wood engraving of 1838 (see p. 17) shows the pies as very small, but being offered from a heated container. What the pies of this nursery rhyme contained it is not possible to determine, but what is certain is that they would be meat pies and fairly certain to have been veal or pork or a mixture of both. The pieman was going to the fair or market on foot, a common sight from the medieval period until the early twentieth century. Go to any fair or large open-air market today and you cannot miss the hot-dog and beefburger stands: savoury meats served between bread, no different from our ancestors' taste, who relished savoury meat served up in a pastry case at the annual market fair. Other than holy days this was possibly the only holiday they were given.

Large pies were produced for the wealthy class, served hot and cold, and pork barely figures as an ingredient. The first recipe of any note for a speciality pie using only pork is published in *The Universal Cook* by Frances Collingwood and John Woolams (1797). This is for an individual Cheshire pork pie, prepared and made in a pie dish. Meat pies prepared in individual pastry cases were always small. The wealthy landowner and squire, if he dared to eat pork in a pie, always expected it to be complemented with other meat. It took a new breed of nobility, the wealthy fox-hunting sportsman, to introduce the large pastry-cased pork pie as a notable dish. The great Hugo Meynell, Master of the Quorn Hounds from the seasons 1753–4 to 1799–1800 revolutionised the sport of fox hunting. He has been given the title 'The Father of Fox Hunting'. In his early twenties he realised, unlike his predecessors and fellow fox hunters, that chasing a fox with a pack of hounds willy-nilly across the countryside may be good entertainment but the real hunting – riding hard, jumping the high fences and deep ditches of the recently enclosed fields south of Nottingham through the Leicestershire Wolds and on to Market Harborough – provided the true excitement of the chase. This resulted in three hunts being centred on Melton Mowbray: Meynell's (The Quorn); The Marquis of Granby's (Belvoir Hounds); The First Earl of Lonsdale's (Cottesmore). By 1800 Melton Mowbray had become the focal point for all serious fox hunters. This was all made possible by changes in national agricultural policy that had resulted in the enclosing awards of the 1760s, which completed the formation of square and rectangular fields, so indicative of the shires, that had slowly spread across the landscape, completing a process that had commenced with the monastic land clearances of the fifteenth century and increased with the Dissolution of the Monasteries and religious houses in the early part of the sixteenth century.

All this coincided with the increase in the number of over-wintering cattle and with the improved methods of feeding cows, so milk yields increased and surpluses occurred, which were converted into cheese. The local cheeses were Stilton and Leicester. Cheese is produced from curds: this is separated from the whey, a liquid that has little or no use except as a superb pig food. With a regular and available supply of cheap food, pig stocks on cheese-producing farms increased, nationally as well as locally, resulting in more pigs being slaughtered, particularly during the autumn and winter months, the fox-hunting season! The 4th Earl of Sandwich's slices of bread and beef may have been acceptable for eating in the gambling clubs of London, but were of little or no use to fox hunters, riding hard across the fields of East Leicestershire. Paper towels did not exist, sandwiches could be wrapped in cloth but were not easy to unfold on horseback, the sandwich could not be placed loose in a pocket. The small purse or parcelled pork pie/pasty made with firm pastry was ideal. A whole variety of types of seasonal pork pie was on

A cottage in the countryside, a wood engraving by Thomas Bewick from a drawing made in the 1790s. A gander is seen attacking the farmer's wife, with the cottage pig foraging in the background.

An engraving drawn by S. Wale from Thomas Hales' *Husbandry* (1756), showing pigs being raised commercially in a farmyard with an automatic feeding system installed. The hopper was filled with farmyard produce and household edible waste.

Thomas Bewick's famous wood engraving of 'The Netty', published in 1797. As a countryman Bewick was making the point that the pig was considered to be unclean only because of its so-called domestication by humans!

offer, produced by farmers' wives for selling on at all the local hostelries. Characters such as the Earl of Wilton, Count Matuscewitz, Lord Gardener, Sir Frederick Johnstone, Lord Rokeby, Lord Forrester and Lord Kinnaird, all 'young bloods', who ate a hearty breakfast and were away across the high fences, carried in their deep pockets superb small oval pork pies. It is said that a Cornish pastie, if it is any good, should stand up to being dropped down a tin mine; equally it could be said that an original Melton Mowbray pork pie should be able to survive in a fox hunter's pocket and should be a delightful snack after over an hour's hard riding.

The first pies/pasties were either purse shaped or made up as a parcel (see p. 15); they were small and easily handled, hot or cold. The small pie that was drawn up as a parcel would most certainly have been packed with jelly, to be eaten cold. The pie shaped like a purse is more likely to have been served hot. The fox hunters operating in and around Melton Mowbray took a liking to the small parcelled pasties, filled with pork and jelly, eaten cold, but they did not travel too well in the cavernous pockets of the hunter's coat. By the turn of the century the small round pie was developed. This was made by filling a glass bottle with warm water and moulding a circle of pastry up and around the base of the bottle to make a small pastry case, the meat mixture was placed in the case, the edges were moistened, a pastry lid was attached, a hole was pierced in the centre and the small pie was baked in the oven. After baking the pies were cooled and gelatine gravy was poured through the hole.

Pork was virtually the only ingredient used to produce this small pie in the district around Melton Mowbray; veal as a filling had declined because of changes in agricultural policy. The production of pork had increased dramatically as a result of the increase in Stilton cheese production. The whey had to be used up somehow, and the simple solution was to feed it to pigs. The fox-hunting fraternity took a liking to the readily available cold pork pies and chose to eat them as part of a main meal – certainly they were served cold for breakfast, and these were much larger pies than those carried in pockets and pouches while hunting. The larger pies again were made by drawing up pastry around circular glass and ceramic jars that had been heated with warm water. As the demand increased the use of glass or porcelain containers was not viable because of constant breakages. The grandmother of John Dickinson, the founder of Dickinson & Morris, is credited with being the first person to draw up pastry around a specially made wooden mould, possibly in the 1820s. The first wooden moulds were round and narrow, not unlike a wooden bottle! It was in this decade that the true Melton Mowbray pork pie developed. In Sir Francis Grant's famous painting *The Melton Breakfast*, commissioned in 1839, large Melton Mowbray pork pies are clearly visible (see p. 17). Pork pies were made by most people who slaughtered pigs, the local cheese producers and many bakers and confectioners. All were for sale at the town market held on Tuesdays and Saturdays, and some of course would supply the local hostelries such as The George, The Bell and The Harborough Arms, along with all the local clubs and public houses supported by the seasonal fox hunters. As with Stilton cheese, the fox hunters who frequented the clubs and hotels of Melton Mowbray particularly enjoyed this locally produced product, and took the pies back to London after the season had finished. The fame of Stilton cheese and Melton Mowbray pork pies spread. Stilton as it aged improved – that could not be said of a pork pie, for it had a 'shelf life' of only a few days! It took the entrepreneurial skills of Edward Adcock, a Melton Mowbray confectioner, to set up the first bake-house on factory lines, producing a Melton Mowbray pork pie which would be retailed outside the environs of the town.

Edward Adcock Jnr ran a bakery next door to the Fox Inn on Back Street (now Leicester Street), baking bread, cakes and pasties for sale by his father in their shop on Nottingham Street. Through appreciative comments on this excellent cold pie, made in the London clubs by returning fox hunters, interest was generated in marketing the product in London. Because it was a perishable commodity and had to be eaten within a few days of manufacture speed in transporting the product was essential. The Leeds to London stagecoach carrying mail passed through Melton Mowbray, arriving in the morning at the George Hotel at 7.45, followed by the London to Leeds coach at 8.15 a.m. Changes of horses and passengers and the delivery and collection of the mail would have taken place at this time, and contact was made with

An autumn celebration of the slaughter of the family pig, an eighteenth-century wood engraving of a typical village scene. Note the child in the foreground blowing up the pig's bladder.

Producing a parcelled pie using a pork mix. This was how the peasant's 'pyez' was made throughout most of the medieval period in England.

one of the guards who frequented the tap room of the Fox Inn. This inn worked in conjunction with the George Hotel, serving the horse-drawn omnibus that arrived from Leicester every weekday morning, and left in the evening at 9.00. The George Hotel, High Street, was a commercial and posting house handling the Royal Mail run by Edward Burbridge, who was the agent for Clark and Phillips, Bankers of London. The Fox Inn, Back Street, was run by Thomas Broomhead. A deal was struck with the Royal Mail guard, appointing a London agent. The guard on the high-speed stagecoach transported the pies to London.

From this small beginning in 1831 developed the nationally recognised savoury pie that is also known throughout most of the western world. For a number of years Edward Adcock had the London trade to himself, but as the reputation of this unique pie spread so did the demand. In 1840 Enoch Evans opened his bakehouse in the Beast Market (now Sherrard Street). So began the great leap forward in pork pie manufacture in Melton Mowbray. By the turn of the century literally tons of pies were being exported from the town, on a daily basis. The opening in 1847 of the Syston to Peterborough railway with its terminus in London was the contributing factor in the increase in the retailing of pork pies from the town. All the major cities of Britain had Melton Mowbray pork pies on offer. It is questionable whether they could all have been classed as the genuine article. In the author's opinion there were pork pies and there were Melton Mowbray pork pies made in the town by 1860!

In 1880 T. Hill & Co. of 103 Belgrave Gate, Leicester, were making a Belvoir pork pie (see p. 104), which was also classed as an excellent local pie. Were they using pigs that had grown fat on the whey produced by the many small farmhouse dairies that were producing Stilton cheese throughout the Vale of Belvoir? Pork pies were manufactured as a cottage industry and in small bakers' shops and by grocers who had the facilities. Edward Adcock ran his pork pie bakehouse for nearly fifty years. Eventually his advancing years forced him to retire, and he handed his business over to his son-in-law William Taylor who was running Melton House Manufacturing in the early 1890s. Taylor started making Melton Mowbray pork pies in his large factory at 26 and 28 Spinney Hill Road, Leicester. So the manufacture of this unique product was leaving the Melton Mowbray area. Taylor's pork pies were not the pies that had been produced by his father-in-law. The pastry cases were made and pressed out by machine, while the meat was prepared as a seasoned mince. These were not the pies of the 1820s, so beloved by the fox hunters of Melton Mowbray.

A true Melton Mowbray pork pie should be produced by raising the pastry around a wooden mould or glass or porcelain jar. The case should be filled with selected cuts of chopped pork, mixed with dried herbs. The mixture should be placed in the pastry case, a pastry lid should be attached to the case by moistening the edge with water, and when secured a hole made in the lid. The sides and top of the case should be brushed with a butter and egg liquid mix, it is then baked in a hot oven, and after it has cooled, gelatine gravy is poured into the hole and allowed to set. The methods used to produce the pastry and meat contents vary with each manufacturer and today are still a closely guarded secret, as they have always been. In the opinion of the author Melton Mowbray pork pies should be made as described, and limited mechanical aids should only be used sparingly: it is a hand-made product. When it is cut for eating, the pastry and jelly must be firm and the meat must be grey in colour with a taste like a good pork chop or well-cooked shoulder of pork. But above all it must be made in the district in or around Melton Mowbray and certainly no further away from the centre of the town than a nineteenth-century packhorse could have travelled conveniently in a day, to market, approximately twenty-five miles. There are excellent pork pies made throughout the British Isles but they are not Melton Mowbray pork pies and should not be labelled as such.

Edward Adcock and Enoch Evans were soon joined by other manufacturers in the 1840s: Mary Manchester and William Whalley on King Street, Henry Roberts and Elizabeth Short on Nottingham Street. In 1851 John Dickinson rented a shop on Nottingham Street which today still produces pork pies and now trades as Dickinson & Morris. This shop had a long history as a bakehouse and confectionery, making bread, cakes and pasties. In 1693 it was sold by John Brocklesby to Edward Basse as a productive

A woodcut of 1820 showing pies being carried to market, used as an illustration to the nursery rhyme 'Simple Simon'.

Simple Simon met a pyeman, going to the fair;
says Simple Simon to the pyeman, let me taste your ware.
This nursery rhyme is thought to have originated in England during the sixteenth century.

A Catnach wood engraving of 1838. Simple Simon is not having much luck!

A pork pie mould, dolly, last, block, or bottle. Developed in the early nineteenth century in Melton Mowbray they were turned out of close-grained hardwood, and replaced glass bottles, jars and ceramic containers.

Sir Frederick Johnstone Bart being served with his kedgeree of kidneys: a detail from the engraving by Charles Lewis of the famous painting *The Melton Breakfast* by Sir Francis Grant, 1839. Melton Mowbray pork pies are on the table to the left of Sir Frederick.

bakehouse. In 1867 Tebbutt and Crosher opened up a pork pie factory in Thorpe End, to be followed by Henry Colin who opened a pork pie manufacturing business in Burton Street.

Advertising in print was in its infancy when Edward Adcock produced the first truly commercial Melton Mowbray pork pie. The quality of the product at that time was communicated by word of mouth. In 1876 the *Family Herald* published a review of a performance of Shakespeare's *Richard III* at the Drury Lane Theatre, in London. A spectator was sitting in the front row of the gallery, the interval was a long time in coming and hunger pangs set in, so he began to unwrap a Melton Mowbray pork pie from his handkerchief. It slipped from his grasp and fell into the centre of the dress circle chandelier, which was lit by gas. As the pork pie began to cook a most appetising odour filled the theatre, distracting the combatants in the Battle of Bosworth scene to such an extent that instead of turning malevolent eyes on each other they were directed to the tantalising smell that was being emitted by the roasting pie suspended above the audience in front of the stage. A comedian in the audience shouted out, to much applause, 'that is a real MELTING Mowbray pork pie'! The report was reprinted in many national and local papers and did much to help in advertising the pork pie trade in Melton Mowbray.

It had become a nationally recognised product by the 1880s when the large Melton Mowbray manufacturers joined forces in an attempt to copyright the pie. This failed, as they were not allowed to copyright the name of the town. There was no historic precedent to fall back on. Although the product had become a recognised food locally and by a few sportsmen nationally by the 1830s, in the 1860s its fame had yet to spread throughout the kingdom. Isabella Beeton compiled and published her famous cookbook *Beeton's Book of Household Management* as monthly supplements through the years 1859 to 1861. In the 1,112 pages of the first edition there are many recipes for making meat pies. This book was compiled for use in fashionable Victorian kitchens, and the Melton Mowbray pork pie is not mentioned – but on p. 394 Mrs Beeton goes into some detail about the making of a hand-raised pork pie, the Warwickshire pork pie. That of course was and is the problem in attempting to copyright a pork pie made in England: pork pies have been made in cottages, farmhouse kitchens and small bakehouses throughout the British Isles for hundreds of years, and all have their own unique recipe and taste. In the author's opinion labelling a pie a Melton Mowbray pork pie – when it is made from a form of salted minced pork, often with other meat or fish added to the filling, and produced in towns and cities situated very many miles from Melton Mowbray – is misleading the public.

As the fame of this tasty pie spread throughout the British Isles so did the demand. From the late 1870s until the turn of the century were the boom years, and the three main manufacturers, Evans and Hill, Tebbutts and Crosher, Dickinson and Colin, cornered the market. During a ten-day period in Queen Victoria's Golden Jubilee year in 1887, these three firms produced 91,000 pies, the majority weighing in at one quarter of a pound. If they were all made at this weight it would have produced a total of over ten tons of pies, but many half, one and two pound pies would also have been produced – an incredible weight and quantity of pies. The Midland Railway Company put on special engines with carriages adapted to convey this vast quantity of pies to all the major cities, London, Edinburgh, York and Manchester among them. Christmas has always been a busy time for pork pie production: in 1907 the local papers reported that the major manufacturers were producing tons of pies daily for the Christmas trade. With the outbreak of the First World War, trade was consolidated, pies being produced to supply the many military camps that sprang up. Unfortunately this war killed the export trade. During the late Victorian and early Edwardian age Melton Mowbray pork pies had been exported throughout the world. In 1890 it is on record that Evans and Hill had received an order to supply a large consignment of their pies to Borneo, considered to be the farthest distance a local pie had been sent until the advent of the aeroplane. These pies were conveyed in the recently commissioned cargo ships used to transfer refrigerated sheep carcasses from New Zealand to England.

There was further decline with some manufacturers closing down during the years of the Great Depression. From the outset of the Second World War the pie became a controlled food, and restrictions

Carrier's cart and passenger, a wood engraving of a drawing by Percy Tarrant, 1889. This was the way most produce was delivered to market. Pork pies were made in village bakeries, butchers' shops, farmhouses and cottages, then transported to market for a small fee by the local carrier. Thomas Hickman, the author's great-grandfather, was a local carrier delivering produce to the Tuesday market at Melton Mowbray, possibly carrying Thomas Oldham's pork pies from Wymondham.

A romantic illustration of the London to Leeds coach in the 1840s. It was because this stagecoach had a terminus at Melton Mowbray that the famous Melton Mowbray pork pie found its way to London. Edward Adcock set up the first commercial bakery to wholesale the pork pie, through a London agent, using the fast daily coach to carry the pies to the city of London. No doubt he also supplied the passengers with this superb snack. They must have been tempted by the savoury smells emanating from the wicker crates used to convey the pies that were securely packed in clean straw.

hit the trade very hard. The large manufacturers never fully recovered, and by the late 1960s only a few baker confectioners were producing the original Melton Mowbray pork pie to the original farmhouse recipe so loved by the fox hunters of the Georgian period. The great producers were in many respects their own worst enemy in deviating from the traditional recipe – they varied the pork mixture to such an extent that this prevented the product being recognised as unique. In the 1980s we witnessed a considerable increase in the demand for a quick midday snack as an easy means of sustenance for the working population. The Melton Mowbray pork pie is on its way back. The industry is again expanding. The pork pie is once more a food for the workers of England as it was for the peasant farmers, hundreds of years ago.

Let's hope the modern manufacturers continue to use a recipe similar to the one developed by the founders of the industry in the 1820s.

The first Stilton Cheese Fair, 1883. This view is of Sherrard Street. From this point to Thorpe End the weekly Beast Market was held. It is evident that it was still considered a market at this time. It was in the Beast Market that Enoch Evans started making pork pies in 1840.

The entrance to Lamberts Lane is on the right. On this corner stands the shop of Thomas Edward Smith, Hatter, Hosier, Outfitter and Fancy Repository. Farther along Sherrard Street on the right stands the Wheatsheaf Tavern run by the Sharman family; they eventually closed this public house and opened a garage on the site, now the central arcade. On the left stands the post office, where George Sanders was postmaster.

A member of the Melton Mowbray fox-hunting fraternity preparing a picnic at the races, *c.* 1850. In the foreground sits a splendid hand-raised Melton Mowbray pork pie.

A horse-drawn coach leaving the Market Place, Melton Mowbray, *c.* 1890. This form of transport was used to convey passengers to the recently opened railway stations and also between other towns in the locality, conveying pies as well as other goods.

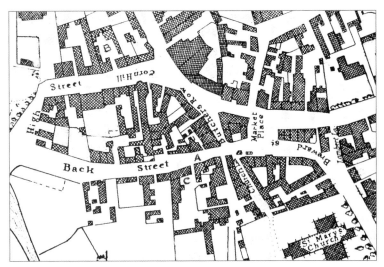

Detail from a plan of Melton Mowbray published in 1839.
A. Edward Adcock's bakery on Back Street.
B. The George Hotel, terminus for the London to Leeds stagecoach.
C. The Fox Inn and yard, the terminus for the Leicester to Melton Mowbray horse-drawn omnibus.

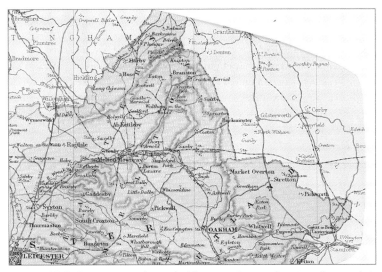

Detail from a map published in 1892. Pork pies had been made in Melton Mowbray and the surrounding district for many decades before Edward Adcock started marketing them. It was he who gave them the name Melton Mowbray pork pies, principally to sell them in London. This unique pie developed in and around Melton Mowbray. When it was first made in adjacent towns and villages, it was conveyed to market for retail, by packhorse or carrier's cart. This map shows the area that could be served by local manufacturers. The outer limits are as far as it would have been possible to deliver pies by horse transport before the introduction of the fast stagecoaches and the steam railway system. Pork pies made at centres outside this plan should not be called 'traditional' Melton Mowbray pork pies. Because of the marketing success started by Adcock and exploited by Evans in the 1840s, competitors sprang up locally, and influenced its distribution nationally. Producers such as Brown's of Peterborough market their own pork pie, the Guildhall pork pie, as do Walker's, with their famous Leicester pork pie; other manufacturers should follow these companies' example and name their products after the area they are produced in, especially when they bear no resemblance to a traditional crafted Melton Mowbray pork pie.

THE INGREDIENTS

FLOUR

Good flour is just as important as good pork in the production of fine meat pies. Flour from wheat has two uses in pork pie manufacture: one, making the pastry, and two, fattening the pig. When wheat flour is ground every part of the seed from the wheat ear is used, producing wholemeal, a coarse flour. To produce a fine white flour the coarse outer bran has to be dressed out, and bran makes a fine pig food.

The first windmill may have been introduced in England by the returning crusaders in the late twelfth and early thirteenth centuries, alongside watermills that had been operating for many centuries. The earliest record of a watermill operating in England is said to be in use at a monastery in AD 762; by 1086 there were 5,624 operating in England, according to the Domesday Book. These mills provided the main means of grinding corn in bulk. Gradually the quern or grinding mill was removed from the farm-house kitchen. This form of grinding corn survived until the end of the nineteenth century in the British Isles, using the system of grinding with two carved pieces of millstone grit, both circular in shape, the bottom stone flat, the top stone often shaped like a beehive, with a pivot and feed hole in the centre and a handle hole off centre (see the drawing on p. 25). Our neolithic ancestors used a much cruder method of grinding corn, a saddle quern (see p. 24).

Pastry making was introduced in the Orient. According to Chinese records they introduced a 'paste' which was made by mixing flour and water. The Greeks and Romans were aware of the mix and added oil and honey. The first form of pastry on record in England was a crude type developed during the early medieval period called 'huff paste'. It was used to wrap around poultry and pork to keep in the juices and to allow the meat to be carried prior to eating. Before the meat was eaten the pastry was removed and discarded; later as flour production and baking techniques improved it was eaten as part of the meal, having absorbed the fat and juices from the meat. In the late medieval period a more palatable pastry was developed, by the addition of pig fat (lard) to the flour. Large filled pies became popular and the small pies developed.

To produce fine flour a dressing unit was an essential feature of all tower windmills. There were two main types, the 'bolter' and the 'wire machine'; the first used an open-meshed cloth to separate the flour, the second used finely woven wire to achieve the same result. Both systems sieved the flour into separate grades. The white flour was bagged for use by the baker; the separated brown bran was bagged to be used as animal and poultry food. Bran mixed with whey is an excellent pig food. Inferior quality corn was also ground and crushed to be used as animal food; this coarser flour was fed to cattle, pigs and poultry.

The local bakers and pie makers would have used flour supplied by the many millers grinding corn in and around Melton Mowbray. Unfortunately as the demand for the Melton Mowbray pie increased so flour production changed. American imports were the main reason for the decline of the local miller. Hard wheat was first grown in the prairies of the USA in the 1870s in a short growing season, as opposed to the long season in England which produced a softer wheat. The American wheat had a higher gluten content and produced better bread; this devastated the wheat-growing and milling economy of the shire counties of the Midlands. The American wheat growers produced large surpluses and this, combined with the new system of rolling corn into flour, rather than the traditional grinding with two circular stones, was the death knell for most millers. Wheat was imported and ground in dockside roller mills. In 1877 the following millers were grinding corn locally by traditional methods: William Barnes (Eye Kettleby watermill); William Cunnington (Coston watermill); Thomas Hayes (Whissendine windmill); William Hives (Asfordby watermill); Thomas Oldham (Wymondham windmill); Frederick Priestman (Garthorpe watermill); Thomas Roberts (Scalford windmill); John Robinson (Waltham windmill).

There were many other millers, as most villages had a mill of some description, and many millers were also bakers. Thomas Oldham of Wymondham was a miller, baker and pork pie manufacturer, fattening his own pigs for slaughter (see p. 114). As the demand for the Melton Mowbray pork pie increased so did the demand for flour. In 1877 Joseph Wyles was milling wheat into flour using a steam-powered mill on Beck Mill Street, as was Henry Smith who ran his Bishop Mill by steam power on Regent Street. Johnathan Bailey had also set himself up as a flour dealer and baker in the Market Place; he extended his bakery business into the manufacture of pork pies, and this continued into the 1960s. These dealers and millers owed their increased business to the expanding pie industry; flour was transported from throughout the county of Leicestershire and beyond. This was all changed very quickly by the influx of cheap American imports of wheat. Many local mills closed down, some struggled on grinding corn for animal feed, but with the development of small steam engines capable of grinding and crushing corn, most farmers processed their own supplies of animal food. The import of US grain meant that most farmers found it uneconomical to grow arable crops and turned their fields over to grazing. The production of milk increased, more cheese was made from the surplus, and the result was greater quantities of whey to fatten pigs. All this coincided with the increase in pork pie production. The staple diet of the 1880s pig was bran and whey. The finer quality American white flour produced excellent pastry, and was much easier to handle than the coarser locally grown wheat flour. These factors working in conjunction with each other helped boost the pork pie industry. The large producers enjoyed three decades of prosperity producing tons upon tons of pork pies.

A neolithic saddle quern of *c.* 2500 BC found at Grange Farm, Wymondham, in 1976.

An engraving of a quern or grinding mill, 1861. Wheat was fed into the grinding system by feeding it into the central hole on the top stone. This stone was loosely held in place on top of the base stone with a wooden stake. The top stone was rotated by gripping the off-centre wooden handle which pushed the stone round; through turning the stone the wheat was ground and the flour fell into the retaining trough. Most large country houses had their quern room until windmills became widespread. These continued to be used where the local milling was controlled by unscrupulous landlords. In some remote areas of the Highlands of Scotland they continued in use until the end of the nineteenth century.

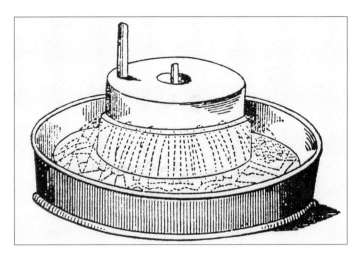

A Bewick wood engraving of the 1790s. Here are the two main methods of grinding corn: the watermill and the windmill.

A development of the small hand-worked quern was the horse-powered flour grinding mill. The same principle applies. It is on record that in 1878 a pig provided the power to a similar mill grinding flour to make pork pies!

A Thomas Bewick wood engraving of the 1790s showing a bakehouse. The dough is being mixed in the 'dough bin' and the baker's assistant is removing bread from the hot oven. He could equally well have been removing hot meat pies.

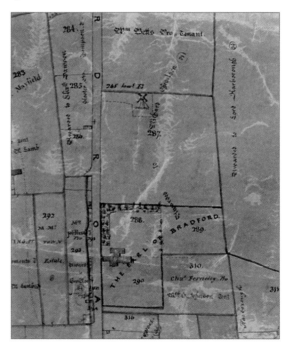

Detail from a plan of the enclosures awards of 1760 for Melton Mowbray. This map was drawn in 1871 and shows the windmill that stood off Scalford Road. In these awards the mill close was granted to Richard Chedelden. By 1850 the mill was being run by Robert Barnes, who was a baker and pork pie manufacturer, though the house, mill and bakehouse were all owned by Richard Hives, who sold them at an auction at The George Hotel on 12 March 1852.

J. H. ROGERS,
Baker and Flour Dealer,
PORK PIE AND SAUSAGE MAKER,
Pall Mall,
MELTON MOWBRAY.

All kinds of Cakes made to order. Bakings carefully attended to, and Families waited on Daily.

Today the manufacture of the traditional Melton Mowbray pork pie is in the hands of a few companies, but this was not the case through most of the nineteenth century. This 1892 advertisement graphically shows how they were made by a variety of producers.

Waltham-on-the-Wolds windmill, 1910. This is a typical tower windmill that produced some flour for pork pie manufacturers during the nineteenth century. Built in 1868 by the Robinson family, it was run by them until they sold it to the Owen brothers in about 1925. For further reading consult *The Windmills of Leicestershire and Rutland* by Nigel Moon, 1981.

Water-powered mills were the main source of grinding wheat to produce flour for the county's bakers. There were numerous watermills operating in the district around Melton Mowbray. For further reading consult *Leicestershire Watermills* by Norman Ashton, 1976. One of the most famous watermills in the county of Leicestershire was the Help Out Mill at Odstone, on the River Sence. Above is a photograph of one of the flour bags from this mill, which was run by the Timms family from 1818 until 1970.

A 'battery' of roller mills at the Spillers mill at Birkenhead, 1898. It was this type of mill that revolutionised the milling industry throughout the world. Joel Spiller, a far-sighted West Countryman, set up in Bridgwater, Somerset, as a corn dealer in 1829. He died as the result of a tragic accident in June 1853 at the age of forty-seven. His business continued and retained his name, growing to become one of the largest flour-milling enterprises in the British Isles.

The development of the roller mill for producing flour in the late nineteenth century changed the industry forever. Many wind- and watermill owners refused to accept the inevitable, and went out of business. Others like the Heygate family took on the challenge of new technology, adapted to it and prospered. This 1950 photograph shows the 'cents' floor of the Heygate flour mill at Bugbrooke in Northamptonshire. This magnificent machine was built by cabinet makers from fine hardwoods, in 1947, on similar lines to machines that were introduced into Britain in the late nineteenth century. Here the sifting system is shown, after the rolling process had taken place: an example of British craftsmanship at its best.

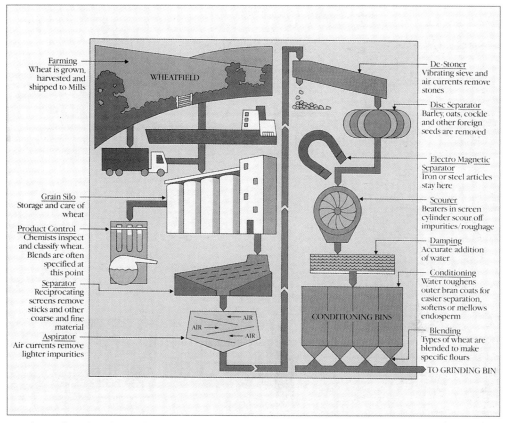

Simple graphics show how wheat is produced and processed to be ground into flour. This illustration and the one at the top of p. 32 were supplied by Spillers Milling Ltd.

The first pork pie pastry case would have been made up very differently from the present day version. Coarse-ground flour would have been used. As technology advanced from hand, water and wind power to the highly efficient roller system of grinding corn that is in use today, so large milling companies started to produce flour for specific purposes. This is the design printed on a sack that would contain Heygates pie flour used in the manufacture of Melton Mowbray pork pies.

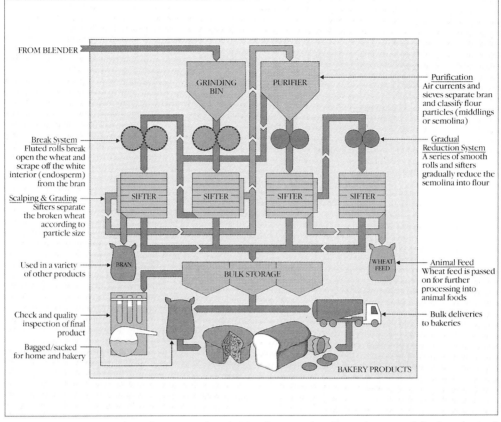

FROM BLENDER

GRINDING BIN

PURIFIER

Purification
Air currents and sieves separate bran and classify flour particles (middlings or semolina)

Break System
Fluted rolls break open the wheat and scrape off the white interior (endosperm) from the bran

Gradual Reduction System
A series of smooth rolls and sifters gradually reduce the semolina into flour

SIFTER   SIFTER   SIFTER   SIFTER

Scalping & Grading
Sifters separate the broken wheat according to particle size

Used in a variety of other products

BRAN

WHEAT FEED

BULK STORAGE

Animal Feed
Wheat feed is passed on for further processing into animal foods

Check and quality inspection of final product

Bulk deliveries to bakeries

Bagged/sacked for home and bakery

BAKERY PRODUCTS

The milling process, or how flour is produced. The diagram also shows that animal feed is obtained simultaneously with white flour production: bran on the left, feed on the right. Both of these ingredients are used to fatten pigs. Flour and pork go hand in hand!

Quality HEYGATES Tells WHEAT BRAN

The success of the Melton Mowbray pork pie in the late nineteenth century was dependent on three factors: plenty of pork, flour and pig food. Surplus whey and the husk from ground wheat are two essential ingredients that fatten pigs, and both were abundant in the Melton Mowbray area. Today bran is still used as animal food as well as being incorporated into breakfast cereals, etc. This is the design printed on a sack that would have been processed at Heygates Mill at Bugbrooke.

HEYGATES

Bugbrooke watermill, Northamptonshire, 1896. There was a watermill on this site when the Domesday Book was compiled in 1086. This undershot watermill was purchased by Mr A.R. Heygate in 1900. The Heygate family had farmed in the area since 1562. A roller mill was developed on the site and this business is still run by the same family. They produce first-rate flour, some of which is used by manufacturers of Melton Mowbray pork pies.

A Heygate lorry being loaded with 140 lb sacks of flour in 1953. Left to right: Jack Dunkley, Jim Nichols, Bill Brown, Alan Perkins, Harry Frost.

Heygate's mill, Bugbrooke, Northamptonshire, 1966. Situated on the River Nene, the nineteenth-century watermill is incorporated into the present building. The mill wheel has been adapted to provide turbo power using water stored in the millpond for generating electricity, if required.

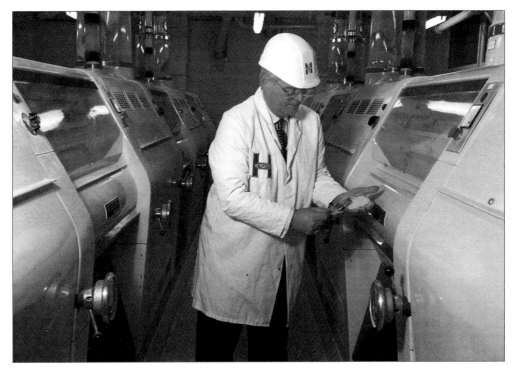

Bob Heygate examining the stock coming off the rollers in Heygate's highly efficient rolling mill at Bugbrooke, 1995. This plant produces a flour that is ideal for making pork pies and other products that require a rich, crisp, full-flavoured pastry, and allows for the absorption of fat so avoiding a greasy taste.

SPILLERS

This photograph taken in 1943 at Birkenhead graphically illustrates the way the flour-producing industry had changed in England at the end of the nineteenth century. Roller mills were built on the docks to process the wheat that was imported from the United States. On the left is a dumb barge used for carrying grain; on the right a smaller vessel is being filled with wheat; centre background shows part of the warehouse and milling complex of Spillers that had been partially destroyed in a German bombing raid – the dockside mills suffered considerably from enemy bombers during the Second World War. Home-grown wheat became very important, one of the reasons that so much surplus grain is produced in the UK. It is a result of improved growing techniques and the more efficient use of farm land, a necessity developed during the 1940s and '50s.

Birkenhead mill, *c*. 1897. The mill had only recently been built.

Spillers Mill on the Trent, Carr Lane, Gainsborough, built in 1958. Wheat was delivered by water, on the adjacent railway systems and by road. Today only road transport is used. The town of Gainsborough has a long history of milling, using the wheat grown on the Lincolnshire fen. During the interwar years many pork pie manufacturers used flour processed in this town. In the dark days of the Second World War Arthur Muggleton, the Somerby baker who produced excellent pork pies, could only purchase his flour under licence from Whitton's of Gainsborough, a company that was eventually incorporated into the Spiller's enterprise. Somerby was the main centre for training the airborne troops who took part in the Arnhem campaign. One of their favourite meals was a Somerby pork pie made with locally raised pork and Gainsborough flour.

General view of the mill yard at Birkenhead, *c.* 1950. Compare this scene with the photograph opposite. Offices have been built in front of the mill; centre left is the engine house with the coal hopper in the centre; to the right is a dock locomotive in steam. Twelve lorries stand in line.

Front view of a steam-powered seven-ton wagon that was in use at Birkenhead in the 1920s.

One of Spiller's Morris Commercial lorries, in use during the 1960s.

PORK

Pigs have been a source of meat for human consumption for over nine thousand years. The pig's ancestor the wild boar was eaten by early man and was possibly the first animal to be bred specifically as a source of food, in China. The earliest known written recipe using pork as meat is in Chinese, dated sometime before 500 BC during the early Chou period. It describes how a suckling pig was stuffed with fruit and herbs, coated with a mixture of straw and clay and cooked in a fire pit. Pork has been one of the main sources of meat throughout the western world and the Orient. During the medieval period in England it was practically the only meat the village peasant ever ate. The Romans of course esteemed pork highly. They also raised other animals as sources of meat, and were familiar with the practice of curing meat, salting and smoking pork. With the collapse of the agricultural economy on the demise of the Roman Empire considerable change occurred in the English countryside, but the raising of pigs and preserving the flesh through immersion in salt continued. It has always been easy to feed the pig, an omnivorous animal; equally it is easy to salt the flesh down, to make bacon. Throughout the Middle Ages the household pig was a crucial source of food. Because it was difficult to find food for the winter, pigs along with most animals were slaughtered during the late-autumn. Only breeding stock was saved. A community would support one boar and a few sows; more often than not these were held by the village squire or lord of the manor, who allocated the piglets when they were born, early in the spring. Well-hung salted pork was essential for survival and was augmented with dried grain, pulses and sometimes turnips stored in cellars or earth and straw 'clamps'.

Rough estimates show the global pig population today to be around five hundred million, roughly one pig for every ten people on earth. In many countries the annual slaughter of the family's pig is still essential for continued welfare. In England the autumn slaughter of the cottage pig died out in the early 1950s, after the lifting of wartime rationing restrictions and with the implementation of government controls, introduced to cover the slaughter of farm animals. During the Second World War the family pig was an essential source of food for the villagers of England; one pig per family was allowed and they all had to be registered with the Ministry of Agriculture. Often second pigs were raised illegally, and the pork and bacon found its way on to the black market that flourished in most town and cities, often distributed by visiting parents of evacuated children who were living in the villages, where they had been introduced to the joys of the annual pig killing and the feast that followed.

A cottage pig often became a family pet. It started life as one of a litter born on a smallholding, farm or even a specialist piggery attached to a cheese-producing dairy. Collected by the man of the house normally on a Saturday morning, in a sack that was slung over his back, the small pig's snout protruded out of a specially cut hole; it would squeal its way home! Most cottages had a pig sty stoutly constructed from brick or stone, containing a small dry room with door and a narrow entrance on to a small gated yard, containing the trough. A kind owner allowed the pig plenty of clean straw and mucked it out regularly, and the piglet was fed wisely in a small trough, progressing to a larger one as it grew.

As it increased in size it always became bored with its prison; its preference would be to forage for food in the woods and heathland, rooting with its powerful snout. This was instinctive and had to be controlled by nose ringing. An unringed pig with its naturally powerful shoulder muscles would soon uproot the most firmly built sty, retaining wall or fence. Usually the village blacksmith would ring the pig using curved horse-shoe nails, although it was possible to purchase special rings that fitted into a purpose-made pair of pliers. A noose of very stout cord was fastened around the upper jaw of the pig, pulled against the noose to draw its head upwards, allowing the curved sharp pointed rings to be pushed through the thick skin at the top of each nostril and then closed with a pair of pliers. This was an excruciatingly painful and cruel process. The rings prevented the pig from 'rooting' for food ever again, because when it lowered its head to engage in what was an instinctive food-searching process the rings ensured that pain was inflicted instantly, stopping the pig in its tracks. Controlled regular feeding was essential; fortunately all household waste food mixed with bran, water and very occasionally whey, was acceptable to a pig. The mixture was boiled to kill all germs, as the death of a pig through incorrect feeding could be a disaster. A life of around eight months was all that a pig could expect, and during that time it would be extremely well fed and pampered, growing large and fat – but come late autumn and its fate was sealed. Normally on a Saturday or Sunday morning the slaughter took place, subject to arrangements with the village butcher. Children and the lady of the house made themselves scarce! It was not a pleasant sight. The author has vivid memories of his very early teens, when he actually helped the local butcher kill the friend he had helped raise throughout the summer months.

The butcher and his assistant arrived; on approaching the sty the pig commenced squealing. With its keen sense of smell it was aware of the blood on the butcher's boots and leather apron. A noose on the end of a short rope was attached to the jaw of the unfortunate animal, which was pushed and pulled to the place of slaughter, a brick-paved area. The terrible squealing was continuous and echoed around the village, a familiar sound throughout the late autumn in most villages in east Leicestershire. A 'scratch' (a wooden ladder-type stretcher on legs) was placed alongside the pig, a humane stun gun was placed in the middle of its forehead, and this pistol was fired projecting a bolt into the skull, using a blank cartridge. The squeals stopped abruptly and the pig was laid on the scratch, its throat was cut and the lifeblood of the animal drained away into a bucket for future use. The carcass was now scraped, buckets of hot water were thrown over the dead pig, all the hair was scraped off the body, and the horns from the toes were pulled from the feet with a hook. The carcass was now spread-eagled on the scratch and all four legs were tied to each handle; it was then opened up, the internal organs were removed (entrails, liver, lights (lungs), heart, kidneys, tongue, etc.), and the bladder was drained and washed then blown up like a balloon to be used for holding lard. This was poured in while it was still hot, using the stem of a tobacco pipe. More often than not the dried bladder was used as a child's football! After the carcass had been cleaned while still tied to the scratch it was propped up against a wall in an outhouse at an angle of 45° for about eighteen hours to drain.

Next day the butcher returned to prepare the hams and flitches. These were salted down in a trough, often a Stilton cheese lead adapted for the purpose. Block salt was specially purchased, crushed, then rubbed with a little saltpetre over the meat. It was essential to rub the salt into the skin until it 'sweated'. Small accidental cuts, inflicted when helping to cut up the carcass, proved very irritating on coming into contact with the salt! The pork then lay in the trough for three weeks; the ham and sides of meat were turned every four days, and brine that drained off the cut-up carcass was ladled continuously on to the ham and flitches. When they had been cured the hams were hung up on hooks fixed to beams in the kitchen, covered with a linen cloth. The sides of bacon were suspended on the walls of the cottage in any convenient spot, covered in muslin to keep the flies off. Many living rooms in country cottages would have large framed photographs of long-dead relatives next to a side of bacon from a recently killed pig on the walls. The bacon and ham was cut as required.

When the butchers trimmed up the hams and the flitches, spare pieces of pork became available, and select portions of this meat were used to make pork pies. This meat was prepared in time-honoured fashion: each house and cottage had its own recipe handed down from generation to generation, with the selection of the pork and the preparation of the dried herbs that were mixed in with the finely cut-up pork being a well-kept secret; this is still the case today. All the traditional pork pie makers in the villages around Melton Mowbray in

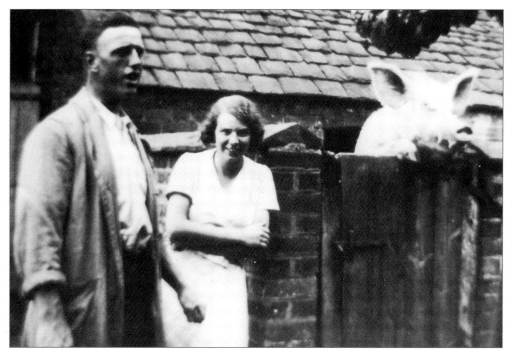

George and Elsie Davis standing outside their pig sty at Houghton-on-the-Hill, *c.* 1935. This scene could have been repeated throughout Leicestershire. Sam the pig was destined to be made into bacon and pork pies. The Davis pork pies were renowned throughout the village.

Fixing a ring in a pig's snout to prevent it from rooting in the sty, *c.* 1940.

the author's youth had their own recipe, as do the traditional manufacturers of commercially produced pork pies today. The same could be said of the pastry preparation. There are only a few traditional Melton Mowbray pork pie manufacturers left, and they guard their recipes well. It is a matter of pride to win a first prize and trophy at the annual fatstock show held in December at Melton Mowbray.

The author's mother used dried thyme and sage that was hung in the sun and occasionally parsley that had been dried in an oven. The dried leaves were crushed and made into a powder; the quantity and mix were never discussed. The quality of the pie always was; the men of the house were often heard to say 'A good pie this, missus'!

Pigs have been bred for thousands of years because they are such an important food supply and varieties of breed are still being introduced. The pig preferred by the author's parents was the English Large White, though many other smallholders favoured other types for a variety of reasons, much discussion taking place on the quality and flavour of the pork. It was no accident that the Melton Mowbray district should have smallholdings and farms raising quantities of pigs. Leicestershire as a county had a long history of pig farming. Thomas Hale, in his extensive agricultural survey of the early eighteenth century that resulted in his book *A Compete Body of Husbandry*, published posthumously in 1756, goes into great detail on the breeding and feeding of hogs. This massive volume of some 750 pages covers all aspect of the changes in agriculture that were taking place as a result of new feeding methods and the introduction of farm enclosures. In the section on pigs he states that 'In some particular counties these creatures thrive better than in others, particularly in Hampshire, Leicestershire and Warwickshire'. So the stage was set for the pig to prosper around Melton Mowbray when increased food supplies materialised owing to the increase in cheese production combined with the increase in milling wheat, bran and whey. The infrastructure was in place, and when it was exploited the manufacture of pork pies expanded to become an integral part of the economy of the town by the turn of the twentieth century. This was helped by the fact that Melton Mowbray had a thriving cattle market dealing in all types of cattle, sheep and pigs. In 1877 William Anderson is listed as a specialist pig dealer trading on Thorpe Road. Many of the cheese makers and factors raised their own pigs and one, Tuxford's, not only produced large quantities of cheese but was also one of the largest pork pie manufacturers in the town.

Today pigs are raised intensively not in cottage pig sties but in open fields where they can root and forage throughout their short lives. A side-effect of an intensive breeding programme has resulted in a breed of pig that has little or no hair on its body, unlike its ancestors. These lightly haired pigs need to have a good supply of water during the summer months to provide mud baths so that they can wallow to their hearts' content, a natural function more important today than it ever was. A coating of mud on the pig's back prevents sunburn, a condition that the modern pig suffers from. Mud is an alternative to factor eight sun block!

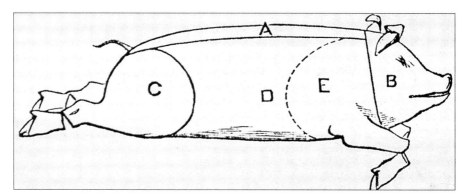

Sectional diagram of a bacon pig: (A) the chine, (B) the head, (C) the leg, (D) the flitch and (E) the shoulder.

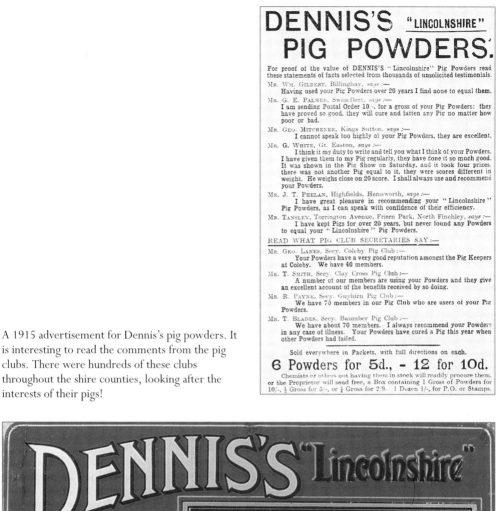

DENNIS'S "LINCOLNSHIRE" PIG POWDERS.

For proof of the value of DENNIS'S "Lincolnshire" Pig Powders read these statements of facts selected from thousands of unsolicited testimonials.

Mr. WM. GILBERT, Billinghay, *says :—*
Having used your Pig Powders over 20 years I find none to equal them.

Mr. G. E. PALMER, Swinefleet, *says :—*
I am sending Postal Order 10/-, for a gross of your Pig Powders: they have proved so good, they will cure and fatten any Pig no matter how poor or bad.

Mr. GEO. MITCHENER, Kings Sutton, *says :—*
I cannot speak too highly of your Pig Powders, they are excellent.

Mr. G. WHITE, Gt. Easton, *says :—*
I think it my duty to write and tell you what I think of your Powders. I have given them to my Pig regularly, they have done it so much good. It was shown in the Pig Show on Saturday, and it took four prizes. there was not another Pig equal to it, they were scores different in weight. He weighs close on 20 score. I shall always use and recommend your Powders.

Mr. J. T. PHELAN, Highfields, Hemsworth, *says :—*
I have great pleasure in recommending your "Lincolnshire" Pig Powders, as I can speak with confidence of their efficiency.

Mr. TANSLEY, Torrington Avenue, Friern Park, North Finchley, *says :—*
I have kept Pigs for over 20 years, but never found any Powders to equal your "Lincolnshire" Pig Powders.

READ WHAT PIG CLUB SECRETARIES SAY :—

Mr. GEO. LANES, Secy. Coleby Pig Club :—
Your Powders have a very good reputation amongst the Pig Keepers at Coleby. We have 40 members.

Mr. T. SMITH, Secy. Clay Cross Pig Club :—
A number of our members are using your Powders and they give an excellent account of the benefits received by so doing.

Mr. R. PAYNE, Secy. Guyhirn Pig Club :—
We have 70 members in our Pig Club who are users of your Pig Powders.

Mr. T. BLADES, Secy. Baumber Pig Club :—
We have about 70 members. I always recommend your Powders in any case of illness. Your Powders have cured a Pig this year when other Powders had failed.

Sold everywhere in Packets, with full directions on each.

6 Powders for 5d., – 12 for 10d.

Chemists or others not having them in stock will readily procure them. or the Proprietor will send free, a Box containing 1 Gross of Powders for 10/-, ½ Gross for 5/-, or ¼ Gross for 2/9. 1 Dozen 1/-, for P.O. or Stamps.

A 1915 advertisement for Dennis's pig powders. It is interesting to read the comments from the pig clubs. There were hundreds of these clubs throughout the shire counties, looking after the interests of their pigs!

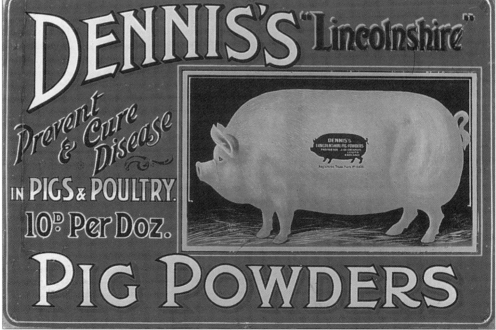

The lid from a tin of Dennis's pig powders.

A modern pig sty built from concrete blocks, *c.* 1970.

Pigs being raised in a yard of straw, 1948.

Pigs wallowing in mud, *c*. 1940.

A modern pig farm of the 1990s in Charnwood Forest, Leicestershire. The policy of raising the pigs free range is clearly demonstrated here. The litter of pigs are enjoying themselves rooting for food. They lead a contented, if short, life.

Bulk storage tanks adjacent to a block of pig sties, *c*. 1930. The tanks hold whey which will be mixed with bran, for pig food.

Two typical scenes from the 1940s associated with many market towns that hold a weekly cattle market. *Left:* pigs being loaded up for market. *Above:* the auctioneer selling each batch pen by pen: the traditional way that livestock is still marketed in England.

A butcher's block that was used to cut up pig carcasses when the animal was slaughtered commercially. Such benches would have been used by the large pork pie producers at Melton Mowbray during the high production years at the end of the nineteenth and the early part of the twentieth century, and were often adjacent to the pork pie bakery.

A Stilton cheese 'lead' used as a salting trough for curing sides of bacon and hams.

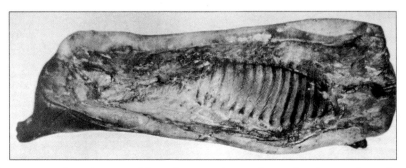

A side of bacon. It was from this part of the pig's carcass that good cuts of pork were obtained to make the traditional cottage pork pie. Today all the best cuts from the carcass are used to produce the commercially manufactured traditional Melton Mowbray pork pie.

These are two pigs that have been bred successfully in Europe and are now found throughout the world. The Large White or Yorkshire (above), bred in England, was considered to be the most widely distributed pig in the world when these photographs were taken in the 1940s. The Landrace (below) was bred in Denmark and was the first breed to be improved by controlled scientific methods. It is now reared throughout the world.

MELTON MOWBRAY

Edward Adcock is credited with being the first confectioner and baker to manufacture for the wholesale trade the famous Melton Mowbray pork pie. He certainly did not make the first pork pie commercially in Melton Mowbray. In the early 1830s the following people were making pork pies in the town as part of their baking and confectionery business: Edward Adcock (Back Street); William Easom (Sherrard Street); Mrs Heaford (Market Place); William Manchester (King Street); George Pilkington (Market Place); Elizabeth Short (Nottingham Street); Lucy Whalley (Sherrard Street); in addition to these there would be village pie makers and casual pie makers who produced seasonal pies as surplus pork became available. Out of town producers would deliver pies in baskets on foot (see the woodcut on p. 17). Producers from further afield would convey their product packed in panniers, strapped to packhorses or brought in the carrier's cart.

It is to the wholesale producers of the Melton Mowbray pork pie that credit must be given for establishing it as an internationally recognised meat pie. Who were the first commercial producers? William Easom could conceivably be considered one of the first. His firm commenced operation as a baker, confectioner and grocer near the Beast Market (now Sherrard Street) in 1790. Many years later, the business transferred to Butcher Row (Cheapside), where Easom's continued to trade until the shop closed in the 1960s, having retained an interest in the baking side of the business from their bakehouse, situated off Thorpe End near the Carnegie Library. There would have been other bakers casually making pork pies when the need arose as a seasonal commodity, particularly during the autumn and winter months; the summer pie was the veal pie. Pork pie making would possibly have taken place in the town during the early part of the sixteenth century, all to be consumed locally. It was Edward Adcock's decision to begin trading in London that started the wholesale distribution of the Melton Mowbray pork pie. His bakehouse was situated next to the Fox Inn yard on Back Street. His father ran his confectionery shop on Nottingham Street, a thriving business, with increased trade generated through the daily deliveries to London on the Leeds to London Royal Mail stagecoach. Business increased and by 1849 Adcock had transferred his bakery to larger premises on Burton End; later he involved his son-in-law William Taylor, who ran a business on Spinney Hill Road, Leicester; eventually Taylor's took over all of the Adcock trade. This Leicester firm continued to produce Melton Mowbray pork pies along with many other types of meat pies; they had become the largest Melton Mowbray pork pie manufacturers in Leicester by 1895.

In 1848 John Dickinson, the founder of the firm Dickinson & Morris, started to make pork pies in a bakehouse on Burton End; a year later he was well established and because of competition and increased trade moved part of his business, taking out a lease on an existing bakehouse on Nottingham Street in 1851, where the manufacture of the famous Melton Mowbray pork pie has continued until the present day. It was no coincidence that Adcock and Dickinson started to make pork pies on Burton End in the late 1840s. In 1847 the Midland Railway line was opened, with the junction at Peterborough, and trains travelled into King's Cross in the heart of London. As with the Stilton cheese trade, the growth of the pork pie industry gathered momentum when the stagecoach was used to convey pies to London and other cities, but it was the railway age that transformed the industry. In 1860 Henry Colin was running a bakehouse at Burton End making pork pies in a yard opposite the Harborough Hotel; by 1880 Colin's business was being run by Joseph Dickinson, a cousin of John. Possibly this yard, and certainly the surrounding area, supported more than one bakehouse, because of the close proximity to the Midland Railway station. The yard and buildings were taken over by Sutton Bros in 1922, and this firm continued to make pork pies well into the 1970s. The Dickinson family had a long association as dealers and producers of pies, and as merchants marketing Stilton cheese, possibly dating back to the late eighteenth century. Joseph Morris was taken into the firm in 1886 as an apprentice from the local workhouse. John Dickinson treated him as a son, making him a partner in the company in 1901, when the name of the firm was changed to Dickinson & Morris. It was in this year that the site on Nottingham Street was purchased. When Joe Morris became the sole owner of the business in 1908 he concentrated on pork pie production, retailing the pies in air-tight containers in specially constructed railway carriages and in the refrigerated holds of cargo ships returning to Australia, New Zealand and South Africa. He lived above the shop and as the business expanded he built a fine house on Nottingham Road, which was demolished in 1933 to build the Welby Hotel. Morris raised his own pigs on his smallholdings in sties laid out in fields almost opposite Sysonby Lodge, Nottingham Road. His head pie maker from 1929 to 1934 was Charles Skerritt. During the interwar years the directors were P. Hudson, F. Harris and M.A. Watson. The company was purchased by Bernard Pacey and George Liston Young in 1950 and run by George Young. A partnership was formed; Pacey owned 49% of the share capital, Mr and Mrs Young 51%. When George Young retired his son David ran the bakery for a number of years. The pork used by the company at this time was supplied by Don Smart's slaughtering business to Jack Browett, the nearby butcher, who selected the best cuts of shoulder pork to be made into Dickinson & Morris pork pies. In 1992 it was purchased by Samworth Brothers and it is now considered by many connoisseurs to be the premier pork pie manufacturer in the British Isles.

Undoubtedly the company that enhanced the reputation of the Melton Mowbray pork pie more than any other organisation in the nineteenth century was the pork pie business started by Enoch Evans at the Beast Market/Sherrard Street in 1840. By 1855 his business was expanding to such an extent that it caused comment in the local newspapers of the era. By this time small bakeries were incapable of meeting the demand, so in about the year 1859 Evans commenced building a specialist pork pie factory on Thorpe End. By 1860 he had sold his business at the Beast Market and had taken into his company James John Hill, his nephew, and so the company of Evans & Hill was formed. The firm was renamed Evans & Co. in 1910, when it was purchased by Henry Morris, Stilton cheese manufacturer. Because of the close association between the production of pork and the manufacture of cheese, Evans & Co. began factoring cheese as well as producing a variety of meat pies. In 1877 they stated that they were the 'Original manufacturers of the celebrated Melton Mowbray, Pork, Veal & Ham and Game Pies'. Unquestionably the visit by the American author and farmer Elihu Burritt in 1863 changed the way the Melton Mowbray Pork pie was viewed internationally. Burritt, whose book *A Walk from London to John O'Groats* was published in 1864, was most impressed when he was escorted around Evans' pie factory. This is the relevant section from his book:

> From Oakham I walked to Melton Mowbray, a cleanly, good looking town in Leicestershire, situated on the little River Eye. I spent a quiet Sabbath in Melton; attended divine service in the old parish church and listened to two extemporaneous sermons full of simple and earnest teaching and delivered in a conversational tone of voice. Melton Mowbray has also a very respectable individuality, it is a great centre for the scarlet-coated Nimrods who scale hedges and ditches in well-mounted squadrons after a fox, preserved at great expense and care, to become the victim of their valour. But this is a small and frivolous distinction compared with its celebrated manufacture of Pork Pies. It bids fair to become as famous for them as Banbury is for buns. I visited the principal establishment for providing the travelling and picnicking world with those very substantial and

The commercialisation of the Melton Mowbray pork pie trade commenced in 1831 in the bakehouse run by Edward Adcock, in part of the building that is now Beano's Restaurant. Adjacent to The Fox Inn, the bakehouse was situated just beyond the entrance on the left-hand side. The original wall still stands and is clearly visible in the photograph, showing considerable wear to the bricks; some of this damage must have been caused by the horse-drawn Melton Mowbray to Leicester omnibus that used this yard as a daily staging post.

Burton End, 1887. Forty years previously the railway station off Burton End was opened, and this radically changed the way in which the Melton Mowbray pork pie was distributed. Instead of using the daily horse-drawn stagecoaches to transport pies to London and other major cities, special carriages were commissioned on the railway system. Edward Adcock moved part of his business to this area and by 1860 Henry Colin was producing pies in a bakehouse shown on this photograph. The entrance to his business was through the arched doorway behind the second tree on the left.

palatable portables. I went under the impulse of that uneasy suspicious curiosity to peer into the forbidden mysteries of the kitchen, which generally bring no satisfaction when gratified and which often astonishes a man not only to eat what is set before him without any question 'for conscience sake' but also for the sake of the more delicate and exacting sensibilities of the stomach. I confess that my first visit to this, the greatest Pork-Pie factory in the world, savoured a little of the anxiety to know the worst instead of the best in regard to the solid materials and lighter ingredients which entered into the composition of this surprisingly cheap luxury. There were points also connected with the process of their elaboration which had given me an indefinable uneasiness in the refreshment rooms of a hundred railway stations. I was determined to settle these moot points once and for all. So I entered the establishment with an eye of as keen a speculation as an excise man searching for illicit distillery, and came out of it a more charitable and contented man. All was above board fair and clean, the meat was fresh and good, the flour was fine and sweet; the butter and lard would grace the neatest housewife's larder, the forms on which the pies were moulded were as pure as spotless marble; the men and boys looked healthy and bright, their hands smooth and clean, their aprons white as snow. Not one smoked or took snuff at his work. I saw every process and implement employed in the construction of these pies for the market, the great tubs of pepper and spice, the huge ovens and cooling racks; the packing rooms, in a word every department and feature in this establishment. And the best thing I can say of it is this, that I shall eat with better satisfaction and relish hereafter the Pie bearing the brand of Evans of Melton Mowbray than I ever did before. The famous Stilton Cheese is another speciality of this quiet interesting town, or of its immediate neighbourhood, so putting the two articles of luxury and consumption together, it is rather ahead of Banbury with its cakes.

Burritt returned to Melton Mowbray in 1867 and was entertained in a most lavish manner by Enoch Evans. He was invited to deliver a lecture in the Corn Exchange; he returned the following year and gave another lecture to a grateful gathering of townspeople. Evans died the following year at the age of sixty-seven. Extracts from Burritt's book were incorporated in Evans & Hill's advertisements (see pp. 61 and 62). In 1877 an article appeared in the *Daily Telegraph* commenting that Evans & Hill's pies were despatched to all parts of the world, leaving Melton Mowbray on the morning passenger trains. Considerable trade was entered into with confectioners in Paris and the British Colonies, and to travel safely the pies were packed and despatched in air-tight containers. In 1892 the company was employing forty people making hand-raised pork pies. In 1914 Evans & Hill were supplying the vast military camp at Belton Park, Grantham, with large quantities of pork pies along with many other types of baked and cooked products from their factory on Thorpe End.

During the summer months trade was slack, so a welcome boost was given when Evans secured the contract to supply the Leicestershire County Cricket Club with pork pies. When the Australian Test team visited the county an order of 10,000 small pies on the first day and 5,000 on the second day was not unusual. In 1910 the business was purchased by Henry Morris, the famous Stilton cheese maker from Saxelby, for £1,300. Evans & Co. bought a main competitor's factory, Colins on Burton End. In 1919, the year that Henry Morris died, the business was run by his three children, Henry, John and Julia, who closed the Colins bakehouse on Burton Street. Sutton Bros purchased the premises in 1922, trading as pork butchers and pie manufacturing. During the Second World War the Ministry of Food applied restrictive measures. Pork was sent to bacon factories. Evans still made pies from other meat. In 1952 the company closed and the then owner/director Miss Julia Morris sold the premises – and in 1963 the famous pie factory was demolished, when a road widening scheme was implemented on Thorpe End.

One of the smaller manufacturers that lasted well into the twentieth century was Warner's, which operated in the Market Place until 1968. Fred Warner took over Adcock's bakery in Leicester Street in 1872, and continued to make pies on the premises until 1884 when he transferred his business to the Market Place, eventually opening up a general confectioners and café. John Pridmore continued to make

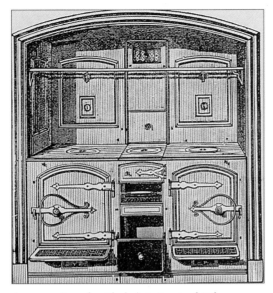

An engraving of a Clarke's Leicester kitchen range, 1880. This is a typical range installed in farmhouse kitchens and small butchers' shops, used for assorted baking purposes, including pork pies.

A small baker's oven used for cooking pork pies in Farrow's butcher's shop on Scalford Road, 1950s. The large producers used purpose-built ovens (see Warner's oven on p. 79).

THE STAPLE TRADE OF MELTON—pork-pies—is about to witness a "new departure." On and after Monday next, our "world-famed dainties" will be offered for sale to the passengers by every train stopping at the Midland station. As to the manufacturers, they are all in it, the arrangement being that each firm, in their turn, shall send down a week's supply. The idea, we believe, has originated with our respected stationmaster, Mr. Bedington, and we wish the project every success.

The railway system allowed Melton Mowbray pork pies to be distributed throughout England. They also became a welcome snack for travellers passing through Melton Mowbray, when according to this report of about 1895 Thomas Bedington, the station master, organised sales of the local pie on the passenger trains stopping in his station off Burton End.

WANTED, a first-class Man as FOREMAN in a Pork-pie Factory; must be steady, capable, and thoroughly experienced.—"P.L.," c/o TOWNE AND Co., Melton Mowbray.

Advertisement placed in the *Grantham Journal* of Saturday 18 September 1897. At this time the three large manufacturers Evans', Tuxford's and Colin's were in keen competition against each other. Obviously one of the companies was looking for an experienced pie maker and did not wish this to become a talking point!

pork pies on the Leicester Street premises until 1909 when the business was sold to Frederick Sharp, whose family continued to run the bakery, making pork pies until 1947 – when it closed after over one hundred years of pork pie production. Fred Warner gained a reputation for supplying pork pies by post, as this extract from Robinson and Pike's *Melton Mowbray* (1892) makes clear:

> Mr. F. Warner, the well-known confectioner and pastry-cook, of Market Place, does quite a brisk trade through the post, orders coming in constantly from all parts of the United Kingdom. This is quite in harmony with the enterprise which characterises the whole of Mr. Warner's business. His large and handsome establishment in the Market Place is one of the best in the district, and both in its position and general arrangements, is eminently adapted for a large trade. The shop is always stocked with a fine selection of pork and other pies, fresh from the bake house; sausages, sausage rolls, tinned vegetables of the leading brands, tinned fruits, fish, American meats, and other choice tinned delicacies, besides high-class confectionery, fancy cakes, biscuits, etc. Special arrangements are made during the hunting season, when so many of the country families and others are continually visiting the town. In the season the best varieties of fruit and vegetables are received fresh daily from Covent Garden, and facilities are provided for supplying lunches, dinners, banquets, etc. The bakeries are completely equipped, and under experienced supervision. Large and all-appointed dining and refreshment rooms are provided on the premises. On market days hot joints and other dishes are especially prepared. The house could not be more conveniently situated than it is, occupying a prominent corner block in the Market Place and within easy reach of all parts of the town.

Competition in pork pie manufacturing grew with the expansion of the Midland Railway system. In 1860 Henry Colin commenced business as a pork pie manufacturer on Burton End (see the photograph on p. 51, which shows the premises built by Colin in 1881, under the direction of Joseph Dickinson). This large building was also used as a maturing room for Stilton cheese. Colin and Co. factored cheese as well as manufacturing pork pies. Young Stiltons were purchased at the cheese fairs, as well as from outlying farm dairies, for eventual transportation along with pork pies in specially constructed carriages on the Midland Railway from the adjacent goods yard and railway station. Henry Colin gained a considerable national reputation as a supplier of pies throughout the United Kingdom. In June 1863 he delivered a thousand pork pies to the Commercial Hotel at Stranraer in Scotland, to be followed in July 1868 with an even larger order, when the company provided five thousand pork pies for the provisions department at the Leicester Agricultural Show. Colin's made all sizes and weights of pork pies; in the same year that the company obtained the contract for the Leicester Show the *Grantham Journal* reported that Colin & Co. made a 29½ lb hand-raised pork pie, which had taken seven hours to bake!

The First World War devastated the export trade for pork pies; to consolidate this local industry Evans & Co. purchased Colins & Co. in 1919, and closed the bakery. Sutton Bros bought the building in 1922 and commenced trading from the premises. Three major manufacturers of pork pies were firmly established in the town by the 1870s. Of these possibly the most successful was Tuxford's! In 1867 Messrs Tebbutt & Crosher, gentlemen's outfitters, decided to change their method of making a living by moving into the expanding pork pie business. In that year they requested local government board permission to build a pork pie factory on Thorpe End, equipped with the most up-to-date steam-powered machinery. As soon as the company started making pies they took into partnership William Thorpe Tuxford of Tuxford & Nephews, Stilton cheese factors in Sherrard Street. The two firms combined and shared the same premises. The pies were traded under the name of Tebbutt & Co., while the cheese was factored by Tuxford & Nephews. They converted part of the premises in 1909 to make Stilton cheese instead of just buying it in from other manufacturers. From 1928 both manufacturing processes were marketed under one company name; Tuxford & Tebbutt Ltd. Production of Stilton cheese and pork pies went hand in hand, especially if the firm was large enough to support its own piggery, using the whey obtained from

CRESTED CHINA

In the 1870s William Henry Goss, a Stoke-on-Trent porcelain potter, encouraged his son Adolphus to market, nationally, china ornaments with city and town crests, as decorative souvenirs. Normally plain white, they carry brightly coloured shields. Other Stoke-on-Trent potters took up the idea, producing many thousands of interesting pieces. These photographs show two porcelain pork pies, with the town of Melton Mowbray's crest embellished on both pies. These were duplicated for other towns with each specific crest displayed on a ceramic Melton Mowbray pork pie, for each town! A unique form of advertising.

A crested china Melton Mowbray pork pie, produced by Swan China, *c.* 1920, carried the verse:

THE MELTON MOWBRAY

Though you travel by train or by liner,
In search of a pie that is finer,
north, south, east or west, Melton Mowbray's the best,
Here's a genuine one, 'Made 'n China'.

A crested china Melton Mowbray pork pie produced by Willow Art China, Longton, *c.* 1920, was enhanced by the verse:

A MELTON MOWBRAY PIE

If a Melton Mowbray Pie
Should ever meet your eye
My advice is hurry up! make haste,
And at once the dainty buy;
Learn why epicures sigh –
Longing for another scrumptious
Non such taste.

the dairy and of course all the waste pastry products from pie making. In 1878 the *Grantham Journal* reported the unusual behaviour of one of Tebbutt's sows. The company coarse-ground some of its own wheat as pig food, and a small grinding mill was built in the piggery, where the pigs were fed: 'The old lady has learnt to grind the corn herself. She takes the handle in her mouth, and moving her head from right to left, manages to grind a large quantity of corn.' Tebbutt & Co. continued to expand and supplied six tons of pies to the Royal Agricultural Show at York in 1883. In 1887 four tons of Tebbutt's pies were sold at the Manchester Exhibition. In 1893 Tebbutt & Co. obtained royal patronage. It was reported in the *Grantham Journal*: 'Messrs. Tebbutt & Co. have purchased a quantity of Royal Pigs and have been favoured with an order to supply a large quantity of pies to Her Majesty's household at Osborne, where the Queen is spending Christmas.' Another good year for the company was 1895: they were awarded the gold medal for pork pies at the Cookery and Food Exhibition in London, followed by the same award at the same event in 1896. The First World War changed Tebbutt's system of pie manufacture: they concentrated their energies on the production of tinned meats and Christmas puddings. The firm continued to make pork pies as demand dictated, only closing down this side of their business in 1966.

Evans & Hill, Colin & Co. and Tebbutt & Co. were the three largest manufacturers of the Melton Mowbray pork pie in the town. The industry peaked just before the First World War, and never fully recovered from the drop in sales that resulted from this conflict. There were very many small bakehouses producing pork pies that ran for a number of years, but they are too numerous to list. Some continued well into the twentieth century. Only one has survived – Dickinson & Morris! Two nineteenth-century small producers gained a considerable reputation as fine pork pie makers. Matilda Batty was making pork pies in her bakehouse in Nottingham Street in 1877. John Sturgess ran a bakehouse in Leicester Street in the 1850s, moving to Butchers Row (Cheapside) in 1855. He traded there until 1870 when Weston & Eckett bought the business. They sold it in 1896 to Henry Wood who continued to make pies on the premises until 1932, when it was sold to the International Stores.

A batch of traditional hand-crafted Melton Mowbray pork pies from the Dickinson & Morris bakery. These pies have been baked unsupported, allowing the fat in the pastry to burn off. Pork pies baked in tins and supported with metal hoops have a different texture and flavour. They are not,.and should never be called, Melton Mowbray pork pies. This pie is classed as the premier pork pie served at buffets and on special occasions, none more so than on 24 October 1944 when the remnants of the 4th Parachute Brigade that had survived the Arnhem campaign, and had trained in the Melton Mowbray area, marched with fixed bayonets to the Corn Exchange near Dickinson & Morris's bakery to be served with specially baked pork pies.

F. SHARP,   THE ORIGINAL
PORK PIE ESTABLISHMENT,
7, LEICESTER STREET, MELTON MOWBRAY.

Letterhead used by Frederick Sharp, who took over the original commercial pork pie bakery at 7 Leicester Street in 1909 from John Pridmore. Pridmore had taken it over in 1884 from Fred Warner, who ran the confectionery in 1872 after Edward Adcock, the founder of the Melton Mowbray pork pie trade, retired. Adcock named the pork pie baked in his bakery 'the Melton Mowbray pork pie' – this was part of his marketing strategy. Pork pies were made throughout England to a variety of recipes, many with additives included in the pork mix, such as other meats and occasionally fish! Adcock's pies were made only from lightly seasoned cut-up chunks of pork. He established the true Melton Mowbray pork pie from recipes handed down from generations of small part-time manufacturers in farmhouses, bakeries, butchers' shops and of course peasants' cottages, where a speciality pork pie had developed in and around Melton Mowbray. Sharp's closed in 1947, and so ended 146 years of pork pie manufacture at the original specialist bakehouse.

Above: Evelyn Sharp standing outside 7 Leicester Street, 1916. Evelyn served behind the counter in this confectioners that sold not only pork pies but also assorted fruit pies, cakes and ice cream (see photograph at the top of p. 51).

Left: Mrs Clara Sharp, 1918. Clara was the head pork pie maker at Sharp's.

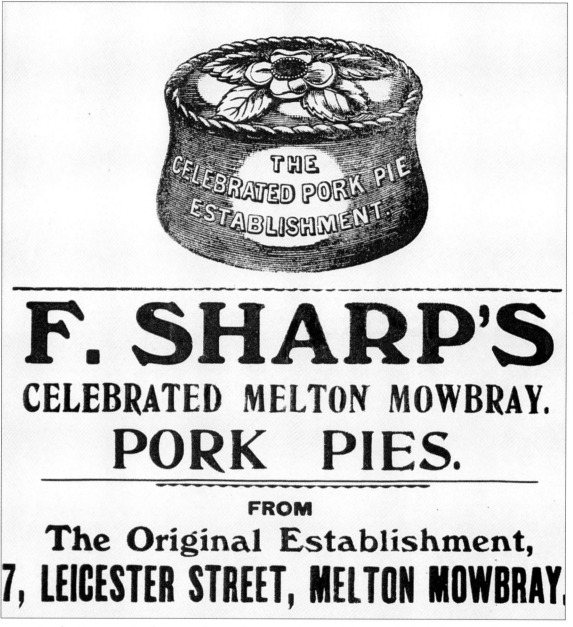

An advertisement printed on greased paper that was used to wrap Sharp's pork pies in the 1930s. For very many years Evelyn Sharp worked in the shop run by her father and as a small child she was often heard to recite the following:

> You take a bit of pork,
> You stick it on a fork,
> You give it to the Jew man Jew!

This rhyme is steeped in time. Traditionally the Jews raised pigs, and made pies, selling them to the Gentiles even though they did not eat the 'unclean' meat themselves.

WOOD

Henry Wood's shop on Cheapside, with bakehouse behind, 1910.

Master baker Albert Brownlow (far left) with his assistants, 1902. This photograph was taken in the yard at the rear of Henry Wood's bakehouse where the pork pies were produced. Albert Brownlow was head confectioner and pork pie maker for Wood's from 1896 to 1932.

Advertisement showing that Henry Wood enjoyed royal patronage in 1911. John Sturgess started the manufacture of Melton Mowbray pork pies in 1855 at Wood's establishment on Butchers Row, later to be named Cheapside. In 1870 the business was purchased by Weston & Eckett, who sold the business to Henry Wood in 1896. Wood's continued to make pork pies on the premises until 1932 when they closed and the shop was purchased by the International Stores who in turn sold it to Halfords in 1977.

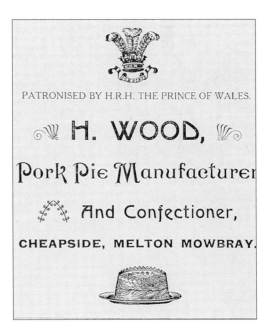

EVANS

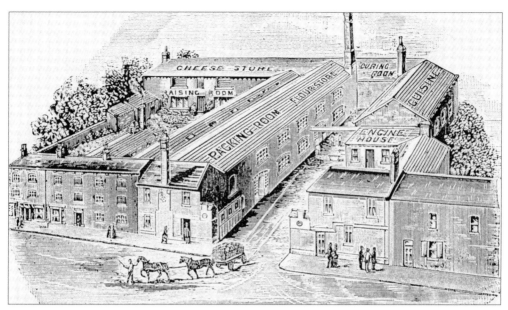

Wood engraving of Evans & Hill's pork pie factory on Thorpe End, 1892. Enoch Evans opened a grocer's shop in Queen's Street in 1830, moving to the Beast Market in 1840. This was where he began making pork pies; in 1859 he started building the factory illustrated above. Opened in 1860, this was the first purpose-built factory to produce Melton Mowbray pork pies commercially.

Enoch Evans with his staff at the factory on Thorpe End, *c.* 1865. Enoch died in 1868, after which the business was run by his nephew James Hill.

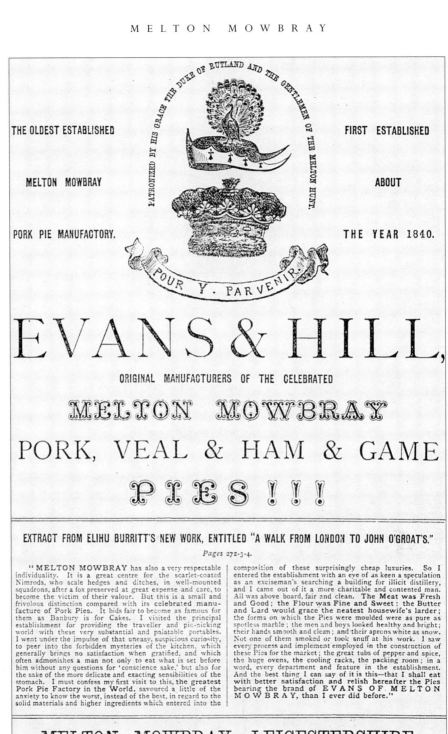

Advertisement published in 1877 by Evans & Hill. Note that they claim to have first produced Melton Mowbray pies commercially in about the year 1840. The advertising campaign began to hot up. That Evans made the first factory-produced Melton Mowbray pork pie was not in dispute; the fact that Adcock was the first baker to market the Melton Mowbray pork pie commercially to a wholesaler in London from his small bakehouse in The Fox Inn yard in 1831 was a very contentious issue.

Evans & Hill advertisement published in 1880. Now they make the claim that Enoch Evans began making pork pies commercially in 1830, one year before Edward Adcock. The advertising war had certainly hotted up! Evans continued to maintain that they had started the business of producing and selling Melton Mowbray pork pies in 1830 until the day they closed their operation in 1952: a slightly misleading statement. Enoch Evans started a retail grocery business in 1830 at the age of twenty-nine.

Staff at Evans & Co. (Melton Mowbray) Ltd, 1910. In this year Henry Morris purchased the business for £1,300. Morris was a prosperous Stilton cheese maker, with dairies at Melton Mowbray, Wymondham, Saxelbye, Stathern, Eastwell and Wymeswold. Henry's dairies produced a considerable amount of whey and he raised large herds of pigs. Evans was a ready outlet for the pork production on his numerous farms. On purchasing the business Henry Morris registered the name: 'Evans original Melton Mowbray raised pie'. Back row, left to right: -?-, -?-, -?-, -?-, Charles Simpson, Steve Barnes, John Barnes, -?-, -?-, -?-, 'Gunster' (a German national). Front row: Gertrude Barnes (wife of Steve, who after his death married Charles Simpson. They had a son Walter who became a butcher at Evans'), Mrs Cole, Lucy Newton.

Henry Morris supervising the workforce at Evans' pork pie factory on Thorpe End, Melton Mowbray, 1918. Henry died in 1919. The business then passed into the hands of his children Henry, John and Julia. Miss Julia Morris ran the operation until its closure in 1952. In this photograph are Mr Meadwell behind the bench on the left, Mr Dobson in front of the bench in a white hat, and Fred Burton next to him.

A cow with one of Henry Morris's pigs obtaining milk direct from the source, at Manor Farm, Saxelbye, 1912. This is near the dairy – note the Stilton cheese cloths hanging out to dry in the background. This photograph hung in the office of Evans & Co. on Thorpe End, Melton Mowbray, and it was considered a suitable subject to be used in promotional advertising. The following verse was written to accompany the photograph:

> This photo tells the truth you see,
> a dainty drink for meat to be,
> no further need of guarantee,
> that Evans' pork for pies shall be,
> from such – this special quality!

Evans & Co., (Melton Mowbray) Ltd.,

(Established 1830)

The Original

Raised Pie Manufacturers,

Melton Mowbray.

TELEPHONE No. 5.   TELEGRAMS: "EVANS, MELTON MOWBRAY."

Left: Logo used on envelopes issued by Henry Morris after he took over Evans' in 1910. Like many of the large pork pie manufacturers, Morris raised his own herd of pigs at Manor Farm in Saxelbye, installing a complicated system of pipes and storage vats to convey the whey from his dairy to the pig sties.
Above: Evans and Co. business card used in the 1940s.

Management staff at Evans & Co., 1943. As a food-producing firm the products of the company were considered part of the war effort, providing much-needed bakery and confectionery for troops and people working in the wartime industries. Back row, left to right: Mr Lane (sausage maker), -?-, Elsie Needham (secretary), Mrs Palmer, -?-, Jack Wyles. Front row: Fred Burton, Percy Medwell (baker), Julia Morris (manager), Mr Woods, Mr Dobson.

Staff at Evans & Co., 1943. Back row, left to right: Fred Burton (chief pastry maker), Ted Fellows, Jack Wyles, -?-, Miss Claydon, -?-, -?-. Fourth row: Mrs Palmer, -?-, -?-, -?-, -?-, -?-, Joan Evans, -?-, Mrs Claydon. Third row: Joan Goodwin, -?-, -?-, -?-, -?-,-?-, Mrs McGarry, -?-, -?-, -?-, -?-, -?-. Second row: Peggy Cox, -?-, -?-, Fred Meadwell, Julia Morris (manager), Mr Dobson, Fred Burton, Elsie Needham, Prue Morris, Joyce Pymm. Front row: Emily Claydon, Miss Marshall , -?-.

Evans & Co. delivery vans, 1946. Left to right: Jack Wyles (butcher), Fred Price, Dennis Wrath, Thomas (Bert) Woodcock. In 1946 Evans & Co. obtained a contract to supply outlets in London on a fortnightly basis: Mooney's Irish Ale houses, the Surrey Restaurant and numerous other retailers. The deliveries were made in one day. Bert Woodcock left Melton Mowbray in the company's van at 2.30 a.m., returning at 7:30 p.m., sixteen hours on the road. On a return journey in 1947, Bert, in van DJU 138, was involved in a road accident at Aylesbury and died of his injuries.

A group of ladies from the packing and pie making departments at Evans & Co., c. 1950. Back row, left to right: -?-, May Mansell. Front row: Julia Woodcock, Mrs Wheatcroft, Mrs Simons. In 1946 the company obtained a contract to supply the workers in the open-cast ironstone mines that were operating in the parishes to the north-east of Melton Mowbray. The special packs contained a pork pie and assorted confectionery made in the bakehouse; they retained this trade for a number of years.

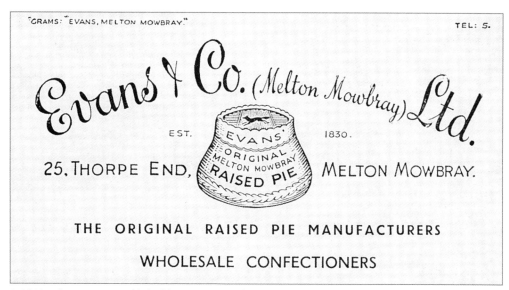

A 1940s advertisement published by Evans. In addition to pork pie manufacturing this company produced a wide range of confectionery products supplying the three cafés they owned: the Blue Room Cafés in Oakham, Melton Mowbray and Leicester.

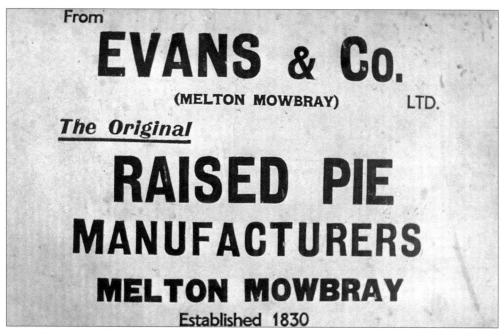

Detail from the side of the standard packing case used by Evans in the despatch of their pork pies, c. 1950. After the Second World War the company enjoyed a short period of increased business. In 1946 George Liston Young joined the company as manager. A native of Scotland, he had reached the rank of captain by the end of hostilities. He arrived at Melton Mowbray railway station in his Highland kilt, much to the surprise of Tony Woodcock, Bert's son, who had been sent by Julia Morris to escort him to the works. George Young left Evans in 1951 and entered into a partnership with Bernard Pacey, a newsagent. They purchased Dickinson & Morris's 'Ye Olde Pork Pie Shoppe' on Nottingham Street.

William Easom's grocers and general provisions shop at 2 Cheapside, Melton Mowbray, 1900. Easom's began trading as bakers, confectioners and grocers near the Beast Market in 1790, certainly making pork pies, transferring to Butchers Row (later to be named Cheapside) between the years 1820 and 1830, when the Melton Mowbray pork pie was coming to the attention of the fox-hunting fraternity.

FARROW

The Farrow family moved to Melton Mowbray from the East Leake area, near Loughborough, in the late nineteenth century. By 1899 Harriet Farrow was making pork pies at their shop at 17 Nottingham Street. She was helped by her son Arthur (Dick) who married Lilian, a maid from Wyndham Lodge. They had two sons, Arthur and Jack. Lilian ran the business after Dick Farrow died, making the traditional hand-raised pork pie until 1952. The butchery business that had now moved to 11 Scalford Road, where this photograph was taken in 1923. In the doorway, left to right, Arthur at the age of thirty-seven with son Arthur aged twelve. The business finally closed in 1960 and the building was demolished in a road-widening scheme.

BEAVER

The staff of Beaver's Bakery, Nottingham Street, 1958. On the stairway, left to right: Len Watts, -?-, Mrs Hedgley, -?-, Elsie Peters, Bert Main. Front row: Mr C. Beaver, -?-, -?-, Jack Vincent, Pat Pick, -?-, -?-, Chris Wildman, -?-.

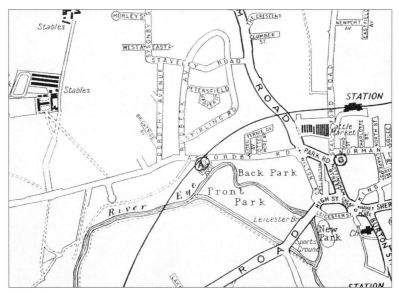

Charles Beaver started making hand-raised pork pies at 8 Scalford Road in 1912. For most of that time Len Watts worked for the company. Len started work there at the age of fourteen in 1923, becoming head baker, a post he held for over fifty years. The bakery finally closed in the early 1990s, though it had long since ceased making hand-raised pork pies. For most of the firm's existence the company raised its own pigs for slaughter. Charles Beaver owned a smallholding on Asfordby Road near the railway bridge. Len Watts lived on this road; he travelled to work on a bicycle and fed the pigs on his way home with waste and 'swill' from the bakehouse. On the plan above (A) marks the location of the pig sties and (B) Beaver's Bakery. In the 1940s considerable change was taking place with the development of council estates off Stirling Road, which meant that the smallholding was soon to be closed down.

BAILEY

Bailey's shop, café and restaurant at 14 Market Place, Melton Mowbray, 1926. This firm was founded in 1867 by Johnathan Bailey who lived with his wife Elizabeth on Leicester Street, close to Edward Adcock's bakehouse. By 1891 Elizabeth Bailey was considered to be a prize-winning pork pie maker.

Bailey, The Pork Pie Shop, 14 Market Place, *c.* 1948. Considerable trade was enjoyed by the Melton Mowbray producers in the 1940s.

R. Bailey, joint owner of Bailey's, 14 Market Place, 1936.

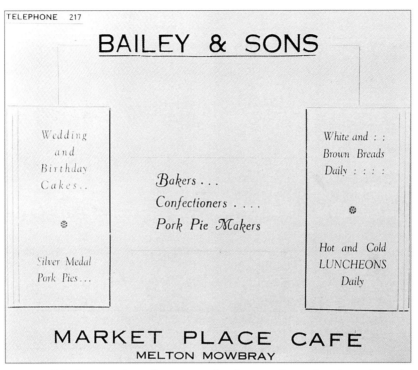

Advertisement published in 1936 for Bailey & Sons of Melton Mowbray. They obviously produced prize-winning pork pies.

F.R. Bailey, joint owner of Bailey's, 14 Market Place, 1936.

Advertisement published for Bailey's Café, 1948. The Bailey family started baking Melton Mowbray pork pies in 1867, and enjoyed considerable trade, having a shop and restaurant in such a prime site in the Market Place. Throughout the years of the Second World War they were able to maintain their service of providing hot lunches. A change in the eating habits of Melton Mowbray businesspeople in the 1960s caused the business to close. Now Curry's occupies the building.

WARNER

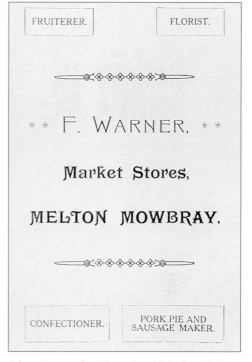

Fred Warner's pork pie shop and general provisions retail outlet with restaurant above, 1892.

Advertisement for Warner's published in 1911.

Warner's had expanded by the time this advertisement was published in 1936. It shows the Market Place premises. They had opened a refreshment buffet at the car park on Wilton Road. This 'takeaway' also provided a service for the adjacent bus station. The author has fond memories of purchasing pies at this shop with his mother, to be taken home for tea and occasionally to be eaten in the bus on the way to their nearby home.

Warner's, Market Place, 1910.

Warner's, Market Place, 1952.

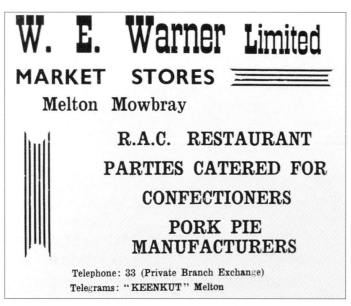

An advertisement for Warner's, now run and owned by William Warner, published *c*. 1940. The business had been started at 7 Leicester Street in 1872, transferring to the Market Place premises in 1884. Considerable expansion took place there; the pork pies were produced in an extensive butchery and bakehouse off Rosebery Avenue. The whole business was sold in 1955 by William Warner to Mr and Mrs Hallam, who continued to produce pork pies until 1962 when the enterprise was sold to Pork Farms. They ran it for one year, then in 1963 they closed down the Melton Mowbray operation and moved pork pie manufacture to Leicester, though by this time Pork Farms were not producing a traditional Melton Mowbray pork pie in any quantity.

Warner's van, Rosebery Avenue, 1933. Left to right: Walter Skerritt (in apron), Frank Warner, Mr Cobley, -?-.

An advertising gimmick was engineered by Frank Warner when Bertram Mills' Circus visited the town and performed on the Play Close in Melton Mowbray in 1933. This photograph shows Walter Skerritt (arrowed) who made a special Melton Mowbray pie for the elephants to eat. Advertised as a hand-raised Melton Mowbray pork pie, the contents were actually fruit cake!

Cutting up pork at Warner's factory, Rosebery Avenue, 1955. Left to right: -?-, John Goodburn, Walter Fowler.

The processing department at Warner's, 1955. Left to right: Tina Bailey, Lucyna Ruzllo, Barbara ?, Anna Wrzyszcz.

Making up pies in Warner's bakehouse, 1955. In this group are Mabel Williams and Nadia Bucka.

Making up pies in Warner's bakehouse, 1955. In this group are Jenny Higgins, Muriel Harker and Ivy Swindler.

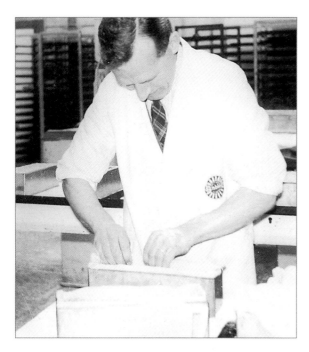

Harry Butler, manager of the Warner's pie factory, Melton Mowbray, making up a 'Gala' pork pie, 1955. These are not traditional Melton Mowbray pork pies. The Gala is a rectangular pie baked in a tin, with a different taste and texture to the hand-raised pie.

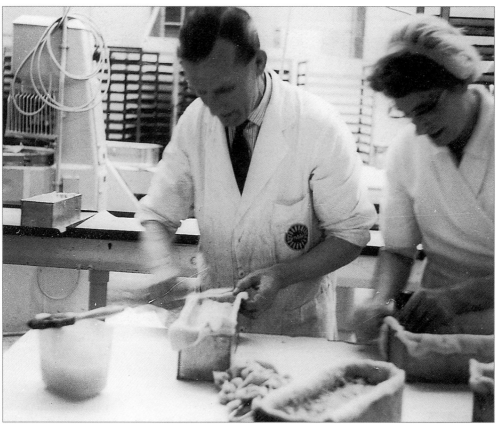

Harry Butler (manager) and Muriel Harker (forelady) finishing off some Gala pork pies, 1955.

Pork pies being fed into the large purpose-built oven at Warner's pie factory, 1955. Ovens very similar to this were used by all the major Melton Mowbray Pork pie manufacturers. Frankie is using a baker's peel to adjust the pies.

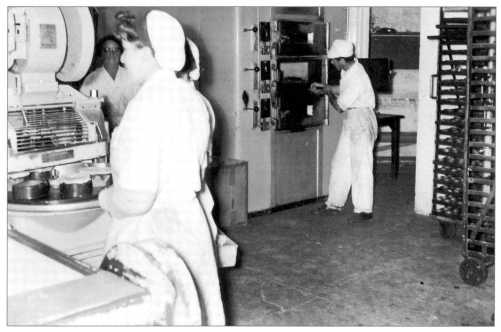

Betty Bishop making pies on a machine, 1955. Warner's gradually moved away from the traditional hand-raised pork pie, and here pork pies baked in tins are being produced. They were a pork pie made in Melton Mowbray, but they were most certainly not a traditional Melton Mowbray pork pie. In the background Frankie is removing pies from a bank of ovens.

Pork pies being removed from the baking trays after cooling before the jelly is poured into the pie. Left to right: Tina Bailey, Mabel Williams, Muriel Harker, Betty Woods.

MARRIOTT

Tom Marriott's butcher's shop produced excellent hand-raised pork pies, 1935. Tom raised cattle, sheep and pigs for slaughter and sale in his own shop, on Nottingham Street. As a local farmer he enjoyed considerable patronage from the farming community, particularly on Tuesdays, market day. His shop was situated only a short distance from the cattle market.

Advertisement for Marriott's butcher's shop, 1936. Tom Marriott opened the shop in 1927; it finally closed its doors in the late 1970s.

Tom Marriott, farmer and butcher, 1936.

Mr P.E. Knipe, manager of Marriott's butcher's shop, 1936.

SUTTON

Benjamin Sutton opened a wholesale and retail business dealing in pork products at 11 Thorpe End, Melton Mowbray, in 1903. This descriptive advertisement was published in 1911.

The Burton Street premises, 1936. The Suttons purchased this building from the Morris family in 1922 and reopened the pork pie bakery which had been built and laid out by Henry Colin in 1881.

Edwin Sutton, 1936. After the death of Benjamin his son Edwin along with his brothers Horace and Wilfred ran the business.

Advertisement printed on a carrier bag used to hold Sutton's products, c. 1960.

Two of the ovens situated in Sutton's bakery on Burton Street, 1979. After 76 years, the business closed on 29 September 1979. At the height of trading Sutton's employed fourteen people.

COLIN

Above left: Colin's butcher's shop retailing pork products at 16 Market Place, 1910.

Above: In 1881 Henry Colin commissioned this magnificent building from which to run his thriving pork pie business. It had been started in 1860, possibly on this site, and was later taken over by Sutton Bros (see photograph of the butcher's shop on p. 82).

Left: The yard of Colin's pork pie and butcher's shop. It was built on Burton End (later to be incorporated into Burton Street), no. 22. In the late nineteenth and early twentieth centuries this would have been a hive of industry: a specialist bakehouse built on the site because of its close proximity to the railway station. Henry Colin gained a considerable reputation for manufacturing hand-raised pork pies. Through the development of specially refrigerated rail carriages the product was transported throughout the United Kingdom. Tons of pies from this outlet were carried to such cities as London, Manchester and Leeds, and a considerable trade in Scotland was generated by this firm for Melton Mowbray pork pies.

TUXFORD & TEBBUTT

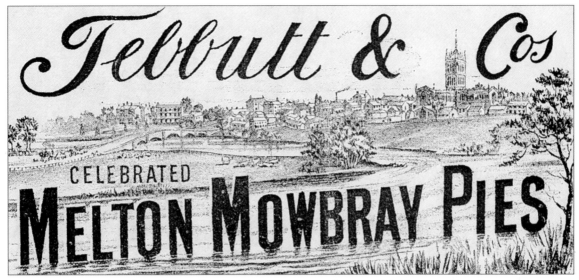

An advertisement for Tebbutt and Co.'s Melton Mowbray pork pies, 1892. The manager at this time was Mr Stevens, and the company was producing 15,000 pork pies per day.

Twenty-four pie makers in the yard at the rear of Tebbutt's factory, possibly in 1895 when the company was awarded the gold medal at the Cookery and Food Exhibition in London. Note the long-handled moulds on the bench, and the dough bin, left foreground.

A gathering of workers outside Tebbutt's pie factory, *c.* 1896. In that year they again won the gold medal at the Cookery and Food Exhibition.

Melton Mowbray pork pies displayed outside the factory along with the workforce — possibly in 1907 when the company celebrated forty years of pork pie manufacture.

Left: Advertisement from 1906. In 1867 Tebbutt & Crosher started business as pork pie manufacturers. Shortly afterwards they took into partnership William Thorpe Tuxford, a Stilton cheese factor. The pies were traded under the name Tebbutt & Co. until 1928 when the Stilton cheese company of Tuxford & Nephews (which had begun making Stilton cheese in 1909) combined with Tebbutt's as one company: Tuxford & Tebbutt. Cheese production overtook the baking side of the business and in 1966 the company closed down the manufacture of all its pork products to make way for maturing rooms for Stilton cheese. *Right*: This is an advertisement published in 1948 when Second World War food restrictions were still in force.

Filling pork pies in the finishing room with liquid jelly, 1960s.

DICKINSON & MORRIS

Left: Dickinson & Morris's Cosy Café confectioner's shop and bakehouse, Nottingham Street, 1912. This shop front has changed little in over one hundred and fifty years. It was leased by John Dickinson in 1851 because the pork pie business was expanding and he needed to diversify. *Right*: Jessie Fellows pouring the liquid jelly into Dickinson & Morris hand-raised pork pies, 1955.

Left: Edward Fellows putting pies in the oven at the Nottingham Street bakehouse, 1955. Ted began working for Evans & Co. in 1916 at the age of thirteen. He joined the staff at Dickinson & Morris in 1950, and retired in 1972. *Right*: In 1951 Dickinson & Morris was purchased by Bernard Pacey and Mr and Mrs Young. Bernard owned the newsagents next door to the famous pork pie shop, and the business was for sale. He needed a skilled pork pie maker, and George Young was leaving Evans & Co. as their head pie maker. George Young ran the business, Bernard Pacey was the sleeping partner. The Corn Exchange, Pacey's newsagents and Dickinson & Morris can be seen in this scene from 1980.

Bernard Pacey, Mrs Veasey and George Liston Young at a presentation evening, 1951. When Bernard died his share of the company was purchased by Mr and Mrs Young.

Eric Routon and Edward Fellows making pork pies, *c.* 1951.

Left: David Young and Tom Cursley making up hand-raised pork pies in the Dickinson & Morris bakehouse, 1976. This is the only pork pie manufacturer now left in Melton Mowbray. The firm was started in the late 1840s on Burton End, shortly after Melton Mowbray railway station was opened. John Dickinson (1828–1908) came from a family with a background in pork pie manufacture. His grandfather was a dealer in a variety of foods, and for a time was a fishmonger. His wife Mary (née Burrows) (1768–1841) was a noted pork pie maker, born in Asfordby, and is credited with the idea of moulds turned out of hard wood to form the pastry cases, as opposed to raising them around bottles or jars. She must be considered the originator of the modern hand-raised Melton Mowbray pork pie. *Right*: In October 1984 Dickinson & Morris were commissioned to make this enormous pork pie. It weighed 85 lb 10 oz. Left to right: Peter Blackshaw (baker) and David Young. The pie was the centrepiece of an exhibition at the Strathallan, Thistle Hotel, Birmingham. The pie contained 45 lb pork, 40 lb pastry and a gallon of jelly and when it was eventually cut up it produced over eight hundred portions.

Making pie cases in the traditional way in the Dickinson & Morris bakehouse, 1980. Left to right: Sally Rudkin, Wendy Parr, Dawn Sanson, Denise Springthorpe.

The Duke of Gloucester samples a Melton Mowbray pork pie in Dickinson & Morris's shop, 1 May 1996.

Traditional hand-crafted pork pies being produced in Dickinson & Morris's bakehouse on Nottingham Street. Left to right: Tony Wensley (placing pies in the oven), Paul Rose, Dawn Sanson, Margaret Lowe (stacking baked pies), Janet Buckle.

Stephen Hallam, managing director of Dickinson & Morris, being presented with the British Baker Marketing award at the gala dinner held at the Grosvenor House Hotel, London, 30 September 1996. Left to right: Bob Monkhouse, Stephen Hallam, Allan Leighton (chief executive of Asda, sponsors of the award).

Congratulations to the team! Dickinson & Morris staff. Left to right: Nigel White, Paul Rose, Sarah Porter, Stephen Hallam, Gavin Green, Margaret Lowe, Chris Beagle, Maureen Pugh, Pat Williams, Dawn Sanson, Pat Ramsdale, Janet Buckle.

Chris Kelly samples a Melton Mowbray pork pie with Stephen Hallam, February 1995. Dickinson & Morris were featured in BBC2's *Food and Drink* programme.

Dickinson & Morris stand at the Burghley International Horse Trials three-day event, 1996. 'The Melton Mowbray pork pie, born and raised in Melton Mowbray.'

Her Majesty the Queen came to Melton Mowbray on Friday 28 June 1996. Buckingham Palace staff requested that Her Majesty should receive a Melton Mowbray pork pie when she visited the town.

Stephen Hallam seals the lid on the famous hand-raised Melton Mowbray pork pie.

A royally decorated Melton Mowbray pork pie presented to Her Majesty the Queen on 28 June 1996. It was specially baked by Dickinson & Morris, the premier Melton Mowbray pork pie bakers, and a leading player in the pork pie trade since the business was purchased by Samworth Brothers Limited in 1992.

THE PERIPHERAL PRODUCERS

U ndoubtedly by 1880 William Taylor's large factory, well established on Spinney Hill Road, Leicester, with its close family connections with Edward Adcock (who continued to make pork pies into the 1870s), can be considered the first factory wholesaler to make and market a Melton Mowbray pork pie outside the immediate town limits. From small beginnings Taylor (Adcock's son-in-law) established an extensive factory at 26 and 28 Spinney Hill Road. A comprehensive account of the company was published in the 1895 issue of *Illustrated Leicester*; an extract is printed below:

Messrs. W. Taylor & Co. The Firm kills its own pigs; indeed, it is the only pie-making firm in Leicester that does this. Lovers of Melton pies – and who are not lovers of them? – may be recommended to pay a visit to the Spinney Hill Road Works, over which we were most courteously shown by Mr. P. Ward, the junior partner. The visitor cannot fail to be struck, not only with the extent of the operations carried on there, and the rapidity with which those operations are performed, but also with the fact that it is impossible that anything in the shape of impurity, or of an unwholesome character, should get into the goods produced. From the slaughter house to the latest process in the packing, every possible care is taken to secure the highest degree of excellence. The sanitary arrangements are perfect, and there is a plentiful supply of pure water everywhere; while a large boiler gives a constant supply, night and day, of hot water on tap. After viewing the slaughter house, the processes and equipments of which are of the most approved character, we come to the sausage and meat cutting room. The rind and the bone are separated from the meat, the fat is taken away, and all that is not required is sold. The meat is chopped or reduced to sausage-pulp according to the use to be made of it by machinery of the latest construction. Sausages of all kinds are made: choice Cambridge, polonaise, saveloys, chicken, tongue, and ham, and German. In the pastry room we find men, youths, and girls, in their appropriate costumes. Pastry-making here is by no means carried on by rule of thumb; it is an art, strictly regulated, and exhibiting an elaborate division of labour. There are, it appears, nine stages in the making of a Melton Pie. The dough is manipulated by machinery, the sheets of pastry having their ornamental devices imprinted upon them as they pass between rollers. The pie cases are constructed, fitted with the prepared meat, ornamented and finished, and then baked in large ovens. A cooling room next receives them, and they are subjected to currents of cold air through valves communicating with the freezing department. Each pie, when ready, is separately wrapped in the registered wrappers of the Firm, and packed in the large packing room. To the visitor, the packing department presents an interesting scene of activity. The chief of the work here is done late in the afternoon, all the Firm's goods being made fresh daily, and sent out on the day of making. The number of hampers – now supplied by the railway company – which are constantly being circulated about the country containing this Firm's goods is enormous. The quantity of goods sent out varies, naturally, according to the season, and according to special demand. The Jubilee year was one of extra activity here; and many thousand pies – including one order for 21,500, from Manchester School Board – being sent out during the Jubilee week. During the same week, the Firm supplied the Leicester Corporation with eighteen thousand buns. It is during Christmas time that the heaviest weight of pies are made. The good old English custom of roast beef and plum pudding for dinner, also recognises that no breakfast table is complete without a Melton Mowbray pork pie. Christmas, 1894, was a record season. Night and day, for over a week, all hands were aloft; and Messrs. Taylor & Co. had the satisfaction of knowing that their pies quite maintained the old-fashioned reputation they started with so many years ago. The success of the Firm is largely due to the celerity and punctuality with which it executes large orders, the Firm having all the conveniences necessary to the prompt execution of orders, in a surprisingly limited period of time. The handsome premises are models of what such premises ought to be, and the management is perfect. Besides the departments mentioned, there are a well-kept engine room and boiler houses, stable and commodious yards in the rear, salt sheds, and a large lard rendering shed, where the gravy for pies is made. The excellently appointed offices are at the entrance.

By 1904 the business had expanded, taking more of the frontage of Spinney Hill Road, nos 20 to 28. The business had in fact peaked by then. The First World War proved disastrous for W. Taylor & Co: by 1916 the company had ceased trading.

One of the well-known names in the county of Leicestershire with a reputation for producing fine pork pies is Henry Walker & Son. Walker's opened a pork butcher's shop making pork pies at 101 High Street, Leicester, in 1880, having started out as a general provisions merchant sixty years previously. The pork pie trade was spreading outwards from Melton Mowbray, so like many enterprising pork butchery businesses they intended to keep pace with the expanding pie industry. By the year 1904 they were well established at 4 Cheapside and 55 Oxford Street; they continued to expand their operation and by 1925 opened a shop at 126 London Road. Like others they encountered problems with trade during both the world wars, but because they had diversified as bacon producers they were not as hard hit as other local pork butchery businesses. They have gone from strength to strength, and are currently considered one of the leading manufacturers of pork pies. Their speciality is the Leicester pork pie, baked in a tin. Occasionally they bake free-standing pies and swept the board at the annual Fatstock Show at Melton Mowbray in December 1995, winning the Roper Challenge Cup for a champion 2 lb hand-raised Melton Mowbray pork pie.

There were many pork butchers and bakers who made Melton Mowbray pork pies in Leicester at the end of the nineteenth and during the early part of the twentieth century. Two other companies gained a high reputation for producing fine pork pies: Arthur Shield in his large premises on 128–130 Belgrave Gate, who also had shops at 36 St Stephen's Road and 24 Wharf Street, and George Wilkinson who operated out of 27 Sussex Street and 27 Granby Street.

In January 1986 the *Stamford Mercury* made a claim that the town of Stamford must be Britain's pork pie capital. This of course was hotly disputed by Dickinson & Morris of Melton Mowbray who had been producing hand-raised pork pies since before 1850 and were still producing them! That excellent hand-raised pork pies were and are produced in Stamford is not in dispute. But those producers came late upon the scene. The pork pie developed in Melton Mowbray because of the coaching trade. As the highways of the East Midlands were improved so the horse-drawn carriage and coach became more widely used. A direct link from Melton Mowbray via Oakham and on to Stamford and the Great North Road existed. Pork pies travel well! The fox hunters realised this, and so did the hostelry owners in Stamford. The recently opened east coast railway line and the petrol-driven bus and car influenced the pork pie trade in Stamford even more in the 1920s. In the development of the industry, locally raised pigs were slaughtered to provide the meat. In the preceding pages the author has indicated how the pork pie developed in north-east Leicestershire, influenced by agricultural changes; the same could be said of Stamford and on to Peterborough and Cambridgeshire; the district did not produce the grain and livestock that it does today. In 1852 Easton and Amos's Appold pumps were used to drain Whittlesea Mere, for modern technology was being introduced to dry out the vast areas of marshland. Within a few years all-the-year-round reliable controls were established, so stopping the annual winter floods, and the Lincolnshire and Cambridgeshire fens became the 'bread basket of England'. Grain produced bran, a prime animal food that pigs thrive on; vast herds of pigs flourished, the Lincolnshire pig trade took off, and so the Melton Mowbray pork pie was adopted in Stamford where it is still produced today using pork from pigs that are raised on the fens.

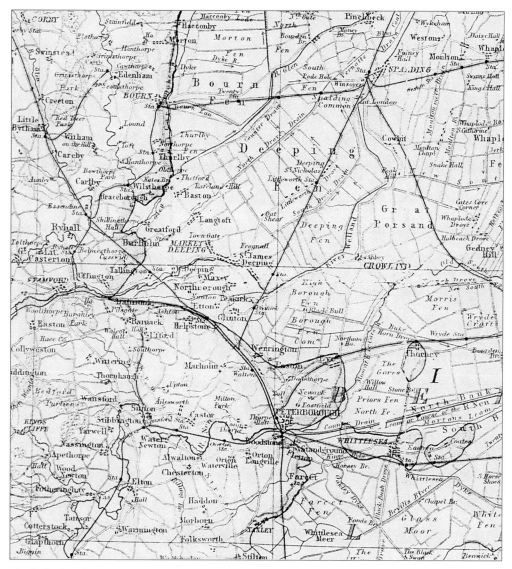

The fenland to the east of Stamford, the home of the Lincolnshire pig, 1876.

STONESBY
BURGIN

This farmhouse was built in 1718, with the bakehouse in the foreground. The Burgin family were running this farm as tenants in the 1760s.

In the kitchen at Home Farm with the utensils used to make hand-raised pork pies. Left to right: scales for weighing out ingredients, wooden butter bowl for mixing the meat, pie moulds and jelly jug.

The bakehouse that stands in front of Home Farm, Stonesby, is unique. It still retains the original stick oven. The building is possibly contemporary with the farmhouse (1718), the present oven possibly dates from before 1850. A stick oven is a very early system used for baking bread and pies. The method is as follows: Fill the oven with dry hedge cuttings (hawthorn), set light to the cuttings and keep adding sticks until the walls of the oven become white, then scrape out all the hot ashes and shut the oven door for five minutes to allow the heat to disperse. If this was not done the tops of the pies always burned. Place the pies on a tray, and put it in the oven. Cooking times would differ: a pie was considered cooked when the gravy began to ooze out of the holes in the lid (there was one central hole with four more spaced around the edge). After the pies had cooled further jelly was poured into the holes to fill any gaps. In front of the oven, left, are a stack of tins used for baking bread by the same process. On the right stands a hay fork for handling the hedge cuttings, a curved rake to remove the hot ash and a metal peel for removing hot pies and bread from the oven.

Left: A stick oven loaded with dry hedge clippings, ready for firing. *Right*: a pie tray holding ten pies was placed in the hot oven. The Burgin recipe for making pork pies was: 14 lb flour, 4½ lb home rendered lard, 1½ pints milk. The lard was heated and the paste made up. The pork was chopped up very fine, salt and a little liquid jelly was added to the mix. The jelly was an essential ingredient to ensure that gravy oozed from the pie when it was cooked, so determining that the pie was ready to be removed. The mix was always prepared in a wooden butter-bowl. Stains from the last baking are clearly visible on the tray. This was made by the gravy oozing and bubbling out of the top of the pies. The jelly was made by boiling pigs' trotters in water.

Left: Joseph and Mary Burgin of Home Farm, Stonesby, *c.* 1935. They raised and killed two pigs each year, principally for salting down as bacon, as did most families living in villages in and around Melton Mowbray. *Right*: Sarah Burgin, 18 June 1994. Born in 1903, Sarah took over the manufacture of the seasonal pork pies in 1920 from her mother Mary, and made them continuously until 1975 using the stick oven. As a rule there were eight to ten pies at each firing, depending on the size of the pies. These pies were eaten by the Burgin family and their farm workers. They were stored in the cool dry farmhouse cellar and would keep for about fourteen days.

PLUNGAR

PELL

The Grange, Granby Lane, Plungar, *c.* 1970. A tractor being driven by Graham Kirk is just leaving the bridge crossing the Grantham Canal opposite J. Pell & Son's butcher's shop and pork pie bakehouse.

A view of the Grantham Canal, with a dinghy upturned on the bank, *c.* 1970. Pell's slaughterhouse stands on the bank with the retaining rails positioned to hold back the cattle arriving for slaughter. Eventually this building was closed, principally because the blood and offal drained into the canal. The bakehouse and the pork pie manufacturing side of the business were extended into this area of the building.

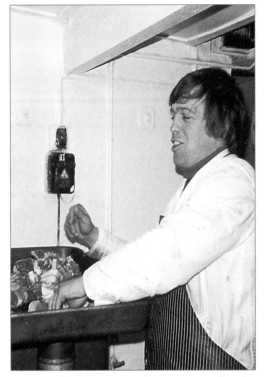

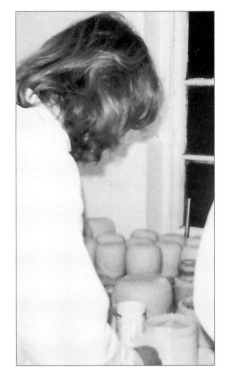

Bruce Rawlins preparing and cutting up pork to be made into hand-raised Melton Mowbray pork pies, 1980.

Elaine Pell making pork pies, 1980.

A batch of Pell's excellent hand-raised Melton Mowbray pork pies, 1980. J. Pell & Son started the butchery business at Plungar in 1898 working out of The Grange, Granby Lane, as butchers/graziers, raising and killing their own cattle and pigs. They had been farmers in the Vale of Belvoir since the late sixteenth century. In the early 1920s they expanded the business to make the traditional Melton Mowbray pork pie, being influenced by Baileys of Upper Broughton and using a similar recipe. The business was closed down in May 1996.

Eve Pell making the pie cases on a wooden pie mould, 1980. Pell's always formed the paste down over the mould instead of working it up from the foot of the block of wood.

J. Pell & Son's delivery van. Left to right: Richard Pell, Simon Watchorn, Bruce Rawlins, in the yard at the rear of Pell's butcher's shop, Granby Lane, Plungar, 1994.

LEICESTER

HILL

In 1863 T. Hill & Co. began making a hand-raised pork pie. In an endeavour to find an alternative to the now quite famous Melton Mowbray pork pie they named it the Belvoir pork pie, a name they managed to register — something that Evans & Hill, Tebbutt's, and Henry Colin's failed to do for the Melton Mowbray pork pie. This advertisement was published in 1880.

SHIELD

A 1925 advertisement published by A. Shield, pork butcher, who had extensive premises at 128–130 Belgrave Gate, marketing, among other products, a traditional Melton Mowbray pork pie.

FOLWELL

G. Folwell & Son, bacon and pork retailers, operated in the Market Place, Leicester, and sold Melton Mowbray pork pies. This advertisement was published in 1901.

DUNMORE

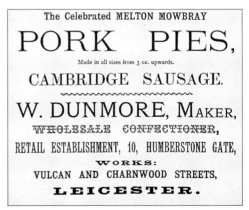

W. Dunmore published this advertisement in 1881. He unashamedly named his hand-raised pork pie, made in Leicester, 'The celebrated Melton Mowbray pork pie'.

WALKER

Henry Walker's butcher's shop at 101 High Street, Leicester. This photograph was possibly taken in the year Walker's began trading from these premises, 1880, the year they started to make hand-raised Melton Mowbray pork pies.

Henry Walker's famous shop on Cheapside, Leicester, adjacent to the Market Place. This is where they retail their famous Leicester pork pies, which are baked in tins and have a unique fluted side.

Ian Heircock hand-raising a pastry case around a wooden dolly at Walker's shop. Walker's make a feature of demonstrating the making of the traditional hand-raised pork pie.

Consolidating a traditional Melton Mowbray pork pie. Ian Heircock has just completed the raising of the case and is filling the pie with chopped lightly seasoned pork. Walker's still make a few traditional hand-raised pork pies as speciality, demonstration and exhibition pies.

OAKHAM

SHARPE / HART

Left: Advertisement for H. Sharpe, whose specialities were home-made products including pork pies, 1909. *Right*: Oakham as a market town was influenced by its near neighbour Melton Mowbray, and traders in Oakham latched on to the pork pie business as soon as it took off in the late nineteenth century. Considerable influence was also generated because of the close proximity of the Lincolnshire Fens and the rapid growth of the Lincolnshire pig trade, as this very descriptive advertisement published by Hart's in 1909 confirms. Many butchers' shops produced hand-raised pork pies in Oakham well into the 1990s.

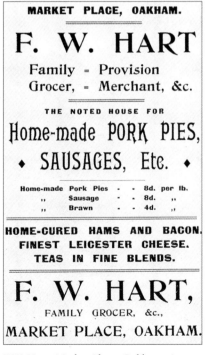

F.W. Hart, Market Place, Oakham. A 'noted house for home-made Pork Pies', 1909.

Dennison's advertisement published in 1909. Today no pork pies are made in Oakham. It is still possible to purchase them in the town (see pp. 128 and 134), but these are hand-raised Melton Mowbray pork pies that are made in Stamford and Whissendine.

UPPER BROUGHTON

F. BAILEY

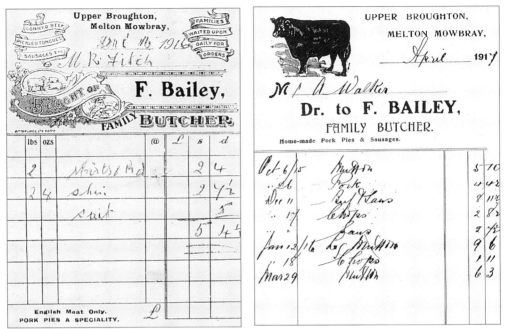

Invoices issued by Fred Bailey, 1916 and 1917. In 1905 Bailey moved to Upper Broughton, having recently purchased the village butchery business from Herbert Woolley. One of his first tasks was to expand the business in the direction of traditional hand-raised pork pie manufacture.

Bailey's butcher's shop, Station Road, Upper Broughton, 1985. In the early years of pork pie making at this butcher's shop the pies were baked in the kitchen range, then as the business expanded they were conveyed in a pony and trap to be baked at nearby Nether Broughton at the extensive bakehouse of Whittakers, one of the two pork pie manufacturers in that village.

Cutting up pork, 1985. This is placed in Bailey's pies which are retailed at shops at Sutton Bonnington, Asfordby, West Bridgeford, Melton Mowbray, Ruddington, Radcliffe, Long Clawson, Plumtree, Thurmaston and Somerby.

Sheila Rowson operates the cutting machine to process the pork prior to mixing, 1985.

Mixed and seasoned pork ready to be placed in the pastry pie cases, 1985.

Paste made from Spillers flour, 1985.

Balls of paste prepared for making into pie cases, 1985.

Traditional pork pies ready to be placed in the oven. Bailey's installed their first oven in 1956: the business was expanding and they needed more control of their product.

Telephone: MELTON MOWBRAY 822216

F. BAILEY & SON

High-Class Family Butchers
PORK PIES AND SAUSAGES A SPECIALITY
UPPER BROUGHTON

M 19

Compare the current invoice heading with those printed on p. 108. Eighty years on F. Bailey & Son are still producing excellent hand-crafted Melton Mowbray pork pies.

Bailey's pork pies being made up, 1985. Left to right: Joan Swain, Lilian Bailey, Jenny Herbert, Betty Whittaker.

Baked pork pies being tested in the modern electric ovens by Jenny Herbert, 1985.

Jack Bailey, who took over the business when his father Fred died, 1985. Jack died in 1989, having worked as a butcher for sixty-two years. He was past National President of the Meat Traders' Association.

Bailey's produce an average of seven hundred pork pies per week, baking on Tuesdays and Wednesdays. This is the production team. Left to right: Joan Swain, Margaret McConnell, Scott Bailey, Betty Whittaker, Anne Copley, Lillian Bailey, Alan Bailey. In this photograph three generations of Fred Bailey's family are featured. Lillian, wife of Jack, Alan, son of William, and Scott, Lillian's grandson. Tradition is important in the production of the celebrated Melton Mowbray pork pie. Its future seems secure at this butchery and pork pie making business.

JONES

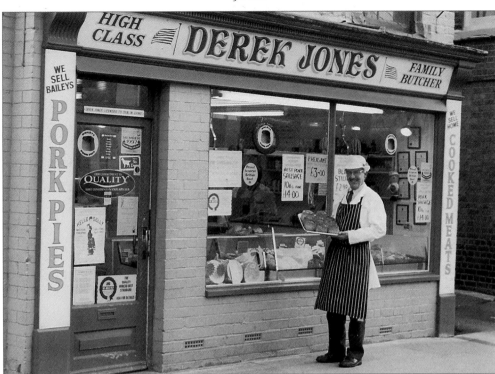

Derek Jones standing outside his shop on King Street, Melton Mowbray, with a tray of Bailey's pork pies.

Advertisement from a paper bag used to wrap Bailey's pork pies.

WYMONDHAM

OLDHAM

Wymondham windmill, built in 1813 by Thomas Compton, and seen here in 1904. It was bought in 1860 by Henry Bowder, who came from a milling family that was also in the butchery business in Lincolnshire. Possibly he built the large bakery and pig sties adjacent to the mill. In 1870 Thomas Oldham bought the mill. He baked bread, raised and slaughtered pigs and marketed pork pies, and the mill remained in the Oldham family until 1952.

In 1988 extensive alterations were made to the outbuildings next to the mill. The large bakehouse oven was demolished. It had been constructed from locally produced brick and the front of the oven was similar in design to this engraving of 1880. It was good business practice to have a bakehouse and raise pigs at a mill site. The pigs were fattened on a diet of flour products and in Wymondham a ready supply of whey was available from the Stilton cheese-producing dairies. Excellent hand-raised pork pies were made there.

TURNER

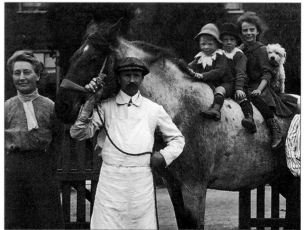

Charles Humphrey Turner's billhead issued in 1910. He ran his butchery business in part of the out-building attached to East Holme off Edmondthorpe Road, Wymondham. Making excellent pork pies, the business was continued after his death by his son Lionel whose wife Nancy was responsible for manufacturing the pies. Lionel died in May 1974: he was the butcher who annually slaughtered the author's parents' pigs.

The Turner family standing with their pony outside East Holme, *c.* 1910. The butcher's shop was situated to the right of the photograph. Left to right: Mary Turner, Charles Humphrey Turner, Charles Richard Turner, John Lionel Humphrey Turner, Phyllis May Turner.

CORBY GLEN / WYMONDHAM
TAYLOR

Thomas Henry Taylor's butcher's shop at Corby Glen, Lincolnshire, 1909. Taylor was a Lincolnshire pork butcher of some repute who had exploited the Lincolnshire pig trade. He moved to the village of Wymondham in Leicestershire in 1912. He purchased land and became a general grazier and butcher.

Left: Dick Bennett, pork butcher, Wymondham, *c.* 1950. Dick eventually set up a business in Boston, Lincolnshire. *Right*: Steve Taylor, the son of Thomas Henry, overseeing the cutting up of a roasting pig, *c.* 1950. Between 1946 and 1953 Dick Bennett and Steve Taylor ran a specialist pork butcher's shop on Edmondthorpe Road, Wymondham. It specialised in excellent hand-raised Melton Mowbray pork pies which were made by Florence Bennett (née Taylor) and Steve's wife, Vera.

NOTTINGHAM
KING

An enhanced photograph of Mrs Elizabeth King's shop front on Beast Market Hill, Nottingham, *c.* 1930. In 1853 Mrs King opened up a shop in Lister Gate, Nottingham, making pork pies as a speciality along with pork sausages and other products. The business prospered, so she moved to larger premises on Beast Market Hill. On her death it passed to her nieces who retained the name. They in turn handed the enterprise over to John Frekingham, later to become sheriff and mayor of Nottingham.

A Mrs Elizabeth King delivery van. When John Frekingham died he was succeeded by his son Eric who entered into a business arrangement with Pork Farms. Owned by Kenneth Parr, this company, which had started in one shop in the centre of Nottingham, grew into a large conglomerate, buying up other pork pie businesses, and concentrating on the mass production of pork pies in tins as opposed to the traditional hand-crafted method. Kenneth Parr sold the enterprise, and in 1980 he relaunched the Mrs Elizabeth King brand, concentrating on the hand-raised Melton Mowbray pork pie.

CROPWELL BUTLER
KING

These are the trade marks of Elizabeth King pork pies. Kenneth Parr decided to make the traditional pork pie using the best ingredients. A bakehouse and shop was opened in delightful surroundings in a glade of conifers in the village of Cropwell Butler in Nottinghamshire. The business is run by two brothers, Ian and Paul Hartland.

Neil and Ian Hartland weigh and make up pastry balls before making the pie cases.

In 1994 Mrs Elizabeth King won the coveted Melton Mowbray Championship for the best hand-raised pork pie at the annual Melton and Belvoir Fatstock Show. Left to right: Paul Hartland, Kenneth Parr, Ian Hartland.

Removing the wooden pie block from the hand-raised pie case.

Neil Hartland pierces the lid of the completed pie; Ian Hartland raises the case around the mould.

Joanne Stanley is filling the pie case with the pork filling made from the best cuts of shoulder pork. Ian Hartland is attaching the lid and sealing the top of the pie.

The speciality of Mrs Elizabeth King is to supply their pork pies made up frozen, ready to be baked in the customers' ovens – a modern concept in pork pie retailing. After the pies are made up they are frozen and packed with clear instructions, ready to be cooked and eaten at home. They can be purchased at specialist food shops and from the small shop at Cropwell Butler. Here the staff are displaying their range of prize-winning pork pies. Left to right: Joanne Stanley, Neil Hartland, Paul Hartland, Ian Hartland.

ASFORDBY
SMART

When Tuxford & Tebbutt closed their pork pie manufacturing department in 1966 some of the plant was purchased by Don Smart of Barkeston-le-Vale. He had been trading in pork pies produced at Langham by Coulthards for a number of years. Here Don Smart is seen examining the recently installed oven at his newly built bakehouse at Asfordby, where he employed eight pie makers, 1966.

Smart's only produced pies for a few years, from 1966 until 1969. On 30 August 1969 a disastrous fire destroyed the premises and it never reopened. However, Don Smart as a councillor on the Melton Mowbray Urban District Council did much to promote the Melton Mowbray pork pie. He was commissioned by the Melton and Belvoir Agricultural Society to standardise a specification for the traditional Melton Mowbray pork pie. It was published on 7 October 1966. This is the specification.

(1) The top may be decorated so as to conceal any holes made during the making, with suitable shapes from pastry.
(2) The pie body to belly out without any support during baking.
(3) The crust to be short and rich, not hard.
(4) The meat to be diced and tastefully seasoned and the stock evenly distributed around the meat. Both fat and lean meat to be evenly distributed.
(5) The pie to be baked evenly to a golden brown.
(6) The flavour is the most important factor, when served cold.

In 1968 Smart's of Asfordby was broken into and a quantity of pork pies were stolen.

STOP THIEF!

Our Pies really are good. But is it really worth it?...

It is so much easier to order through the usual channels

SMARTS PORK PIES

Telephone ASFORDBY 261

SOMERBY

ASHBY

Henry Ashby's butcher's shop, Main Street, Somerby, *c.* 1920. Excellent pork pies were retailed from this shop. Left to right: Alf Houghton, Mrs Ashby, Henry Ashby, Mr E. Lee, Nell Wade.

Ashby's butcher's shop, Somerby, *c.* 1950.

MUGGLETON

The Old Bake House, High Street, Somerby, was built in 1765. In 1940 Arthur Muggleton became the village baker, and joined forces with Edgar Lee, the village butcher. These two tradesmen combined their skills, which led to the first truly commercial pork pie making enterprise in the village. The pigs were killed in the local slaughterhouse, the pork was prepared and then taken to the bakery where the pies were made up. The traditional hand-raised Melton Mowbray pork pie made in Somerby gained a considerable reputation during the years of the Second World War and shortly after. Pork pie making ran in the Muggleton family. May Ann Muggleton was known as 'The Pie Maker'. When a cottager's pig was killed she was called in to make the pork pies, which were then cooked at the village bakery.

Arthur Muggleton, baker, delivering bread and pies, March 1947. This was at the height of the great freeze when Somerby, like so many villages, was cut off from the outside world for many weeks. Self-sufficiency was the order of the day. On the right is Arthur's bakehouse.

QUENIBOROUGH

Butcher's shop, Queniborough, 1909. Left to right: Stafford Mansfield (butcher), Katherine May Mansfield, Katherine Mansfield, Stafford Mansfield. Seasonal hand-raised Melton Mowbray pork pies were on sale in this shop. Around 1947 the business was run by Ralph Bramley, who made and sold hand-raised pork pies.

CLARKE

Clarke's butcher's shop, 27–29 Main Street, Queniborough. These are the premises shown in the above photograph; excellent pork pies are retailed from this shop to the owner's recipe, baked in Thurmaston.

WHISSENDINE
FORRYAN

Nick Forryan is rolling out the pastry to produce the lids for the hand-crafted pork pies. This is the bakehouse on Main Street, Whissendine, Rutland, with the company's range of moulds standing in the window.

John Forryan attaches the lids to the traditional pork pie, *c.* 1960.

Completed pies being placed in the Baker Perkins oven by John Forryan, *c.* 1960.

Finishing off a hand-made pork pie in Forryan's bakehouse, Whissendine, *c.* 1960.

John Forryan removes the baked pies from the oven, *c.* 1960.

THORPE END   'PHONE 244
MELTON MOWBRAY and
SCALFORD

Nov. 15   19**32**

M_r_ _J. E. Clarke_

BOUGHT OF

C. J. FORRYAN & SON

Family Butchers and Tripe Dressers

Charles Forryan opened a butcher's shop at 30 Thorpe End in 1910 and began to make the traditional hand-raised Melton Mowbray pork pie. Henry Morris had recently purchased the nearby large pork pie factory of Evans and Co., and both businesses used a similar recipe. In 1926 the business expanded to run a shop at Scalford, trading as Forryan and Sons. The pie shops were expanding because of the quantity being sold; the bulk of the orders were baked at Lambert's bakery at Wymondham.

Forryan's butcher's shop on Main Street, Whissendine, _c._ 1960. John Warwick Forryan closed the Melton Mowbray and Scalford businesses down and in 1940 consolidated his company at Whissendine, having moved to this village from Melton Mowbray in 1930, and so starting to make his famous hand-raised pork pies in Rutland. He used pork obtained from pigs raised on a farm at nearby Pickwell.

John Thorpe with the Christmas display at Forryan's butcher's shop, 1960. Shortly after this photograph was taken John, a superb butcher, set up in business at Wymondham opposite the Berkeley Arms on Main Street.

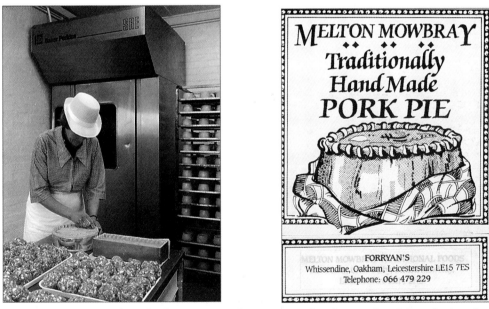

Left: Anne Forryan completes the decoration on a large supported pork pie with a Gala pork pie to her left, 1990. Balls of seasoned pork stand in the foreground waiting to be placed in the traditional hand-crafted pie cases. Completed traditional Melton Mowbray pork pies stand on racks in the background waiting to be baked – made from the finest pork and Rank Hovis flour. *Right*: The display package used to carry the famous Forryan 1 lb pork pie, *c*. 1970. During the last seven years this has been declared the best 1 lb pork pie at the East of England show at Peterborough on three occasions, and taken the second and third spot on two other occasions. With local government reorganisation Forryan's are now situated in Rutland. Today Forryan's are solely wholesale suppliers, delivering their pork pies to retail outlets throughout England.

ATKINSON

Sheila Atkinson standing on the steps of Whissendine General Stores with Forryan's pork pies that have been baked in Forryan's bakehouse a few yards from her shop. You cannot purchase Forryan's famous pies direct from the producer, but it is possible to purchase them in the village of Whissendine, the home of the Forryan pie.

GRANTHAM MEAT COY

Paul Miles, manager of the Grantham Meat Coy shop, 31A High Street, Oakham, holds a tray of Forryan's hand-crafted Melton Mowbray pork pies made in Rutland.

MICHAEL'S

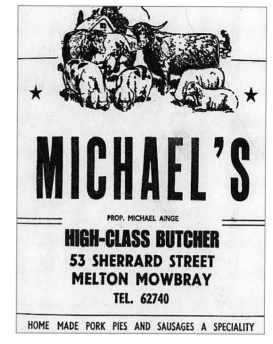

An advertisement printed on a paper bag used to wrap Forryan's 1 lb pork pies. These were sold on Sherrard Street, a few yards away from the site of Forryan's original shop on Thorpe End, Melton Mowbray.

Michael Ainge standing in front of his shop with a tray of superb hand-crafted Melton Mowbray pork pies, baked in the time-honoured fashion, unsupported. The traditional bellying of the pie is clearly visible. This is the sign of a true Melton Mowbray pork pie made by Forryan's of Whissendine, for sale in Melton Mowbray.

STAMFORD

HALL

C.W. Hall, 8 Red Lion Square, *c.* 1920. The Lumby family were running a butchery business from this address, 1820s – 1860s. From 1863 to 1872 Mary Stickson was in charge of a specialist pork butcher's shop and provisions dealer. This was probably when the first pork pies were made on the premises. The shop had a number of owners after Mrs Stickson. Mr Hall bought it in 1894, about the time of this photograph. He appears to be making a pork pie in a tin, a 'Stamford pork pie'. In 1924 Harold Nelson purchased the business.

NELSON

Left: Harold Nelson was awarded the silver medal for his pork pies at the Cookery and Food Exhibition in London on 11 November 1927. Nelson's speciality was pork pies; he produced a 'Stamford pie' in a tin and a hand-raised 'Melton Mowbray pork pie' in Stamford. The company continued to win prizes and consistently exhibited superb hand-raised Melton Mowbray pork pies at the annual Fatstock Show at Melton Mowbray.

Right: Harold Nelson must have been a supreme pork pie maker. In 1927 he was awarded this splendid diploma for his pork pies by the Confectioners, Bakers and Allied Traders' Association. There were numerous pork pie manufacturers in Stamford in the period between the two world wars. Nelson's were the largest producers. Most of the Stamford pork pie manufacturers baked them in tins or hoops, so these were not Melton Mowbray pork pies.

Nelson's shop, on the corner of Broad Street and Ironmonger Street, 1991. One of Nelson's refrigerated vans is parked at the side of the shop. The company has three mobile shops delivering into Rutland, Lincolnshire, Cambridgeshire and Northamptonshire.

Nelson's pork pie bakery, Alma Place, Stamford, 1960. In the foreground Beryl Garwood is pouring the jelly into traditional hand-crafted Melton Mowbray pork pies; to her left are four trays of 'Stamford pork pies' that have been baked in tins. Both are produced by Nelson's. In the background, left to right, are: Arthur Houghton, Jon Bell, Richard Davis, Jack Parker, Reg Ramm.

Inside Nelson's Broad Street shop, Stamford, 1957. Charles Dutton (left) is seen with Johnny Palmer.

Nelson's shop, Red Lion Square, Stamford, 1991. Brian Gelsthorpe (left), and Matthew Naisbitt.

Advertisement printed on the paper bags used to carry pork pies. Note Nelsons are approved by the EEC. They have complied with the bureaucracy, while many pork pie manufacturers have not and have gone out of business.

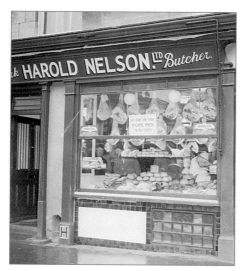

Nelson's shop, Red Lion Square, 1957.
Compare this photograph with the one of Hall's
shop at the top of p. 130.

Harold Nelson Ltd, 12 High Street East, Uppingham,
1957.

Vernon Stokes stands in the doorway with a tray of
Nelson's pork pies at the Uppingham shop.

Stephen Powis, manager, stands outside the Red
Lion Square shop, with a tray of Nelson's pork pies.

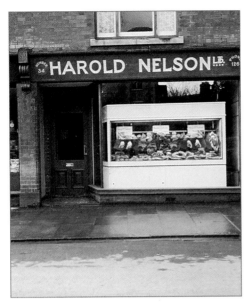

Harold Nelson Ltd, 34 High Street, Oakham, one of the three Nelson's branches that traded in the town at this time, 1957.

Nelson's, 26 High Street, Oakham. The shop manager, John Cook, stands in the doorway with a selection of hand-raised pork pies.

The production staff from Nelson's factory stand in the forecourt at Alma Place, Stamford. This fine selection of decorated traditional hand-raised Melton Mowbray pork pies would have graced the breakfast table of any fox-hunting gentleman who lived in Melton Mowbray in the nineteenth century. Left to right: Alan Wyles, Robin Horsley, Mick Fox, Trevor Harries, Darren Towell.

John Watson, manager at the Broad Street shop, Stamford, holds a tray of fine traditional pork pies.

FANCOURT

Geoff Tilley cutting up pork in Fancourt's butcher's shop on St Mary's Street, Stamford. Only the best cuts of pork are used in the making of the pies. The bucket on the floor holds clippings of pig skin and pieces of bone that are boiled to produce the jelly/gravy that is poured into the cooled pies, after baking.

Connie Cox and Sandra Burbeck hand-raise the pastry around wooden pie moulds. Fancourt's use a cold-water paste made from Heygate's flour. Flour and a little salt are placed in a bowl; the lard that has been rendered on the premises from the fat linings from the pigs processed in the butcher's shop is cut up into very small cubes and placed in the flour and salt mix. The three ingredients are mixed together thoroughly. Then sufficient cold water is added to produce a paste of the correct consistency.

Rob Porter removes the baked pies from the oven. Fancourt's produce approximately three hundred traditionally hand-raised Melton Mowbray pork pies per week.

Kevin Roberts pierces the lid of the baked pies as they are cooling before pouring in the liquid jelly.

Left: Mr Jessie Fancourt started making traditional hand-made pork pies in the premises at 33 St Martins Street, in 1904, a boom period for pork pie production in Stamford. This family business was purchased by the Andrew family in 1979. In 1992 the present owner Phil Andrew took over the running of the business. He places great emphasis on quality and the home-grown product. Lincolnshire is famous for its pigs. Phil selects his from Robinsons of Helpston in the Fen: specially raised pigs, fed on a waste biscuit product, to increase the fat yields. These pigs are slaughtered in the company's own licensed abattoir at Grantham. *Right*: Kevin Roberts stands in the doorway of the company's shop with a tray of Fancourt's pork pies.

BROWN

Harry Brown's butcher's shop, High Street, Stamford, Christmas 1923. Richard Brown was running a butcher's business at King's Cliffe near the Great North Road in 1870, fattening cattle and pigs on the recently drained fen at Whittlesey. His son Harry set up in business in Stamford, taking advantage of the expanding market at that time for pork products. The firm started to produce the traditional hand-raised pork pies that they continue to make in their bakehouse in Peterborough. In 1937 this magnificent half-timbered building was demolished, but it was purchased by John Kirk and reassembled at the Castle Museum, York, where it is now one of the main features.

PETERBOROUGH

BROWN

Frederick Brown, one of Richard Brown's sons, opened up a shop in Peterborough in 1916 on the Long Causeway. In the 1970s the city centre was redeveloped and in October 1981 'Butcher Brown' moved to the present premises, 7–8 Church Street, Peterborough.

In 1981 the business was being run by Michael Brown, Richard Brown's grandson. Today the business is still being run successfully by the founder's great-grandsons under the directorship of Matthew W. Brown. In the doorway stands Paul Phipps, holding a tray of Guildhall pork pies, a product of Peterborough.

Brown's of Peterborough are included in this book because they still occasionally make the traditional hand-raised Melton Mowbray pork pie, mainly a seasonal product for the Christmas trade. They began making them in Stamford in the 1920s and still as traditional butchers carry on producing these excellent pork pies. In this photograph Tom Brown is in the process of hand-raising the pie case. He controls the mould with his chin and brings up the paste with his hands. In the bakehouse at Brown's butchery shop all types of hand-made meat pies and pasties are produced.

Tom Brown inspects a tray of Guildhall pork pies. These are not hand-raised pork pies: they are Peterborough pork pies and should not be confused with the Melton Mowbray pork pie, although Brown's still produce these. The butchers and bakers of Peterborough could not have been involved in the development of the traditional hand-raised Melton Mowbray pork pie – they are situated too far away. In any case, they have their own unique product.

RECIPES & RECIPIENTS

Meat pies of various types have been made for thousands of years throughout the world. The pie of England developed during the Saxon/Norman period of our history. The protection and presentation of meat in a retaining protective case is as old as cooking itself. The Polynesians living in the Pacific Islands still cook pork by wrapping it in a case of clay and straw, and place the parcel in a pit of hot ashes to cook. It is not so many years ago that it was common practice for travelling gypsies in Britain to wrap dead hedgehogs in a parcel of clay and cook them in a camp fire.

From wrapping pork in clay and cooking the parcel, to wrapping pork in a rough wholemeal flour pastry was an easy development. Our Saxon ancestors produced the first crude cold pie by baking pork wrapped in 'huff' pastry in pit ovens. When cooked and cooled the parcel was an easily carried package of cooked meat; the ash-covered pastry was discarded. With the addition of spices to the meat before covering it with pastry, the taste was improved, and the juices were absorbed into the protective hard-crust pastry. This became an integral part of the cooked package and was eaten with relish. Instead of covering the pastry-covered meat parcel with hot ashes, the pastry-wrapped seasoned meat was cooked in a separate chamber over the pit or at the bottom of the pit in a pile of very hot cobbles and could have been wrapped in cabbage leaves (see the photograph at the top of p. 143). So the first pie evolved, along with a rough type of baking oven. Crude meat pies were made from poultry and pork in this manner and possibly changed little in a thousand years. This type of cooking is hardly ever mentioned in medieval writing on cooking, simply because it was an everyday occurrence, familiar to the peasant population of England, but little used by the educated and wealthy minority from which came the only scribes. The presentation of the written word was to change in the fifteenth century with the invention of printing from movable type. Caxton printed the first book in English in 1476. Books covering cookery techniques were printed over the ensuing centuries, but pork does not figure largely in these writings; where it does it is normally presented as a meat for the serving class and when it is incorporated in a pie it is always presented with other meats and fish for the nobleman's table.

In 1685 Robert May published *The Accomplisht Cook or the Art and Mystery of Cookery*. He was obviously familiar with the making of hand-raised meat pies. May compiled a number of recipes involving pork; in this collection he also included a number of recipes incorporating separate pastry cases. One type of pastry was made by taking 'three quarters of flour', 'three quarters of a pound of butter', 'boil the butter in fair water, and make up the paste hot and quick'. A pork pie was made by filling a prepared pastry case with chopped pork layered with cooked rings of tongue; into the layers of pork and tongue was added a mixture of powdered nutmeg, pepper, salt and sage, and a hole was made in the lid of the uncooked pie. After baking, hot butter was poured into the hole, filling up the pie case. It was then dusted with flour and served cold. This was a pie made in a nobleman's kitchen.

Richard Bradley FRS, Professor of Botany at Cambridge University, published his important work *The Country Housewife and Lady's Director* in two parts: Part I in 1727, Part II in 1732. That he is familiar with meat pies is obvious. He does not publish a recipe for a pie made solely from pork, but he recommends a special pastry for meat pies: As for Meat Pyes, or Pasties, which is made thus. Rub seven pounds of butter into a peck of flour, but not too small; then make into paste with water.

When cooks working in the large country and town houses used pork in a pie, they inevitably incorporated other meats, and did not use pig fat (lard) in the pastry. It took the wealthy fox hunters residing in Melton Mowbray to demand a simple seasoned pie made out of good cuts of pork. They introduced this superb local dish to the country at large, and in time it became a nationally recognised pie.

It was a pie made in farmhouse and cottage kitchens to recipes that had been handed down by word of mouth for generations. It was, and should be, a simple pie made from pork, seasoned to the taste of each individual cook or baker. Four recipes are printed below; the author leaves it to the reader to decide which is the best.

1860s recipe for pastry

To make pork pie crust,

3½ lb flour.
2 teaspoons baking powder
3 good teaspoons salt

Rub all together, letting the flour be warm and dry, with 1¾ to 2 lb of Lard rubbed in the flour, mixing with warm (not hot) water to a very firm dough. This makes six pounds of dough. (Be sure not to make it too soft.) Mould into wooden blocks the size you want the pies. If you use 2 lb dough (lid included) use 1¼ lb of meat (previously seasoned).

Bake this size 1½ hours.

1930s recipe

Ingredients: 1½ lb lean pork, 1 onion, salt and pepper. For the crust for raised pies: 1 lb flour, 6 oz lard, 1 gill water, salt.

Method: Remove all bone and gristle from the meat, and put all in a saucepan and cover with cold water. Bring to the boil, skim, add the onion, season with salt and pepper, and simmer gently for 2½ to 3 hours. Remove the meat from the saucepan, cut it in dice and sprinkle with salt and pepper. Boil the lard and water together for a few minutes, add to the flour, with which a good pinch of salt should be mixed; stir till sufficiently cool to knead. Work till perfectly smooth, cover and stand in a warm place or by the fire for ½ an hour. Knead the paste again, set aside sufficient to make a lid, and raise into a round form. Fill with the meat, moisten with a little of the stock made from the bones, etc., cover with the lid, press down the edges, make a small hole in the middle of the lid, and surround it with pastry. Brush the whole with beaten yolk of egg, mixed with a little milk, and bake for about 2 hours. Remove from the oven and pour in the remainder of the stock, which should be re-heated.

1950s recipe

Ingredients for pastry: Sift 10 oz plain flour and ½ teaspoon salt into a warm bowl, make a well in the centre and keep in a warm place. Heat 3 oz lard and ¼ pt water together gently, until boiling, then add them to the flour, mixing well with a wooden spoon, until cool enough to knead with the hands. The pastry must be raised or moulded while still warm. Reserve ¼ for the lid and leave in a bowl in a warm place covered with a cloth.

A Saxon fire pit/hearth, *c.* 450. Was the first Melton Mowbray pork pie baked in such a fire pit? This one was uncovered in an archaeological rescue dig on the proposed site of a new bakery to be built by Samworth Brothers Limited off Leicester Road, Melton Mowbray. Pork was wrapped in crude flour pastry and placed into the pit of pre-heated cobbles and cooked accordingly, possibly protected with leaves to prevent the pastry from burning; equally if no protection to the pastry was provided the burnt pastry was discarded before eating the cooked pork.

A 1990s kitchen, where frozen unbaked hand-raised pork pies can be baked according to instructions provided by the manufacturers – a modern method of marketing pork pies. Compare this Neff oven system with Mrs Beeton's kitchen range on p. 145. This is a twentieth-century concept in kitchen design, marketed at 4 Nottingham Street, Melton Mowbray, a few doors down from Dickinson & Morris, pork pie manufacturers, where cookers are displayed by Jane Barnard in a Moben Kitchens shop, on the world-famous pork pie thoroughfare.

Roll out the remaining pastry to about ¼ inch thickness in a round shape. Gently mould over a jam-jar (or pie mould). Grease and flour the jar, invert it, place the pastry over the mould, the pastry round the sides. Take care not to scratch the pastry and ensure that the sides and base are of an even thickness. Leave to cool.

When cold, remove the pastry from the jar and put in the filling. Roll out the ¼ of pastry reserved for the lid, damp the rim and press the edges firmly together.

Ingredients for filling: 1 lb lean pork, powdered herbs, salt and pepper, ½ gill stock. Cut the meat into a small dice and season to taste with herbs, salt and pepper. Place the bones, finely chopped onion, salt and pepper in a saucepan with the water or stock and simmer for 2 hours, so that the gravy when cold forms a firm jelly. Put the filling in the pastry case and cover with a pastry lid. (The remainder of the stock should be reheated and added after the pie is baked and still hot.) Brush the top of the pie with milk and make a hole in the centre. Bake in a hot oven 425°F or gas mark 7 at first; reduce heat as soon as pastry is set to moderate 350°F or gas mark 4 for about 1½ hours.

1970s recipe (extracted from an advertising book for 'Cookeen', prepared by Diana Short, head of the Cookeen Cookery Service)

10 oz plain flour sieved together with ½ level teaspoon salt
1 egg yolk, standard
3 oz Cookeen
¼ pint water
Beaten egg white to glaze
Oven: Preheat to fairly hot ((400° or gas mark 6), middle shelf

Method
1. Have ready a greased baking sheet and a pie mould or a straight-sided container 4 inches in diameter, and double thickness greaseproof paper to tie round pie.
2 . Sieve flour and salt into bowl. Drop in egg yolk and just cover with flour.
3. Heat Cookeen and water together in saucepan and bring rapidly to boil.
4. Immediately pour boiling liquid into flour. Beat with wooden spoon until well mixed and smooth.
5. Put on floured table top and knead thoroughly with fingertips into smooth round ball with no traces of egg remaining.
6. Sprinkle with flour and place in polythene bag. Leave to rest in warm place for 20–30 minutes.

How to make a raised pork pie by moulding

1. Roll out two-thirds prepared pastry dough evenly to around 12 inches in diameter.
2. Dredge upturned straight-sided container 4 inches in diameter with flour. Lift pastry dough on to rolling pin and place over container. Mould dough round container by pressing firmly to sides and keeping edge even.
3. Cut double thickness greaseproof paper to fit round pie. Wrap paper round pastry and secure with string.
4. Leave in cool place to become firm.
5. Turn container upright and carefully ease away the container from paper-wrapped pastry case, twisting gently to loosen. Place on prepared baking sheet.

Sage, thyme and parsley as illustrated by Mrs Beeton in 1861. These herbs were dried and crushed, then very small amounts were placed in pork mixes for Melton Mowbray pork pies, along with salt and pepper – the only additives that should be mixed with the meat in this unique pie.

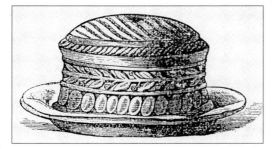

A decorated hand-raised pork pie served at a huntsman's table for breakfast in the 1880s.

A decorated cottage pork pie of the 1980s.

The Leamington stove as recommended by Mrs Beeton, used extensively in the kitchens of the nobility from the 1860s until well into the twentieth century. With its two large ovens it was ideal for baking pies.

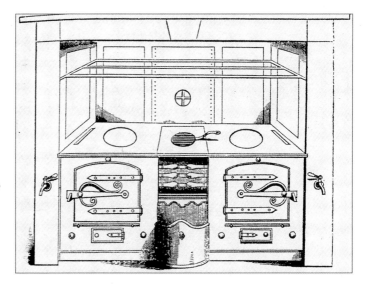

6. Fill with prepared meat mixture, packing it well down at sides to hold the shape of the pie. Brush edge of pastry with water.

7. Roll out remaining third of pastry dough to a circle large enough to fit top. Place on top of pie and press edges together to seal.

8. Trim away surplus pastry and paper, using scissors.

9. Cut a cross with a sharp knife in centre of pie. Fold back pieces. Brush all over top with lightly beaten egg white or water.

10. Roll out pastry trimmings. Cut out four pastry leaves and a decorative bud. Use to decorate the centre of the pie and to fill the hole. Brush with beaten egg white or water. Bake as directed.

How to make decorative bud

1. Mould small piece pastry into small ball.

2. Roll out two small pastry rounds large enough to cover ball completely. Secure loose ends together firmly and turn ball so that ends are underneath.

3. With sharp knife, cut a cross through top of pastry rounds and ball nearly to bottom. Open out and turn back cut segments to complete the bud.

The pie filling

1¼ lb lean boneless pork, cut into small pieces
3 tablespoons stock
¼ level teaspoon dried sage
Salt and pepper
Beaten egg white, to glaze
Jelly to pour in pie after baking
Pre-heat oven to fairly hot (400° F or gas mark 6), middle shelf.

1. Mix meat, stock and seasoning together.

2. Fill the pie case with mixture. Cover and decorate with remaining pastry. Glaze with beaten egg white.

3. Bake in pre-heated oven for 30 minutes. Lower the heat to moderate (350° F or gas mark 4), cover pie with greaseproof paper and cook for further 1¼–1½ hours.

4. Remove paper and allow to cool.

5. Make jelly.

6. With a sharp pointed knife, remove decoration. Pour in the cooled jelly using a funnel. Replace decoration and allow to set. Serve cold.

Jelly/gravy kettle, 1861.

Selecting a ball of paste and the dolly is the start of the process. This series of photographs (pp. 147–52) was taken in Dickinson & Morris's bakery at Melton Mowbray.

Flattening the ball of paste and positioning the dolly.

Drawing the paste up and around the dolly.

Completing the forming of the pastry case around the dolly.

Removing the pastry case from the dolly.

Shaping the pastry case.

Filling the pastry case with chopped seasoned pork.

The filled pastry case.

Attaching the pastry lid to the filled pie.

Crimping the edges of the pie, to hold the lid in place.

The completed pork pie with holes pierced in the lid.

Six traditional hand crafted pork pies, baked ready for filling with jelly.

LONDON
THE MELTON MOWBRAY

The Melton Mowbray Ale and Pie House, 18 Holborn, London EC1.

Karen Day serving the two specialities of the house, Melton Mowbray pork pie served with pickles, salad and a roll, and the alternative, pickles, salad and chips.

Half a traditional Melton Mowbray pork pie, ready for eating and well presented in a traditional public house. Edward Adcock began marketing Melton Mowbray pork pies to a wholesaler who retailed the pies to inns and hostelries throughout London in 1831. You can still eat this excellent pie in the heart of the city today, 166 years later, and they are as good as they ever were.

Menu prepared by the managers of this excellent public house, Jimmy and Hayley Weir. This inn is owned by Fuller Smith & Turner, Griffin Brewery, Chiswick.

STONEPITS FARM

Stonepits Farm on the Salt Way, Wartnaby, Melton Mowbray, originally built in about 1750 as two cottages on infill in a stonepit. Ironstone had been excavated on the site from the Roman period until the 1950s when ore was conveyed to the iron smelting works at nearby Asfordby. In 1993 Janice Musson decided to open a restaurant and tea room specialising in home cooking and local products. The Musson family have a long tradition in local foods, for the present owner's great-grandmother Mary Eliza Musson was a famous Stilton cheese maker – see p. 89, *The History of Stilton Cheese*, Sutton Publishing, 1995.

Kerry Phipps eating a Dickinson & Morris traditional Melton Mowbray pork pie, featured on the Stonepits Farm restaurant menu. Pork pie and Stilton cheese go hand in hand and in this restaurant they maintain the tradition, serving fine hand-raised Melton Mowbray pork pies and superb Stilton cheese as main ingredients in their specialist salad dishes.

SCALFORD HALL

Scalford Hall, the home of Major William Dixon Mann-Thomson, 1915. Built in 1908, this is a fine example of an Edwardian hunting lodge, constructed by a wealthy fox hunter. In 1944 the hall was purchased by Lt-Col. Colman OBE of Colman's Mustard who lived in the hall until his death in 1969. Lt-Col. Colman hunted with the local hunts and promoted his famous mustard as a complement to the equally famous Melton Mowbray pork pie.

Scalford Hall, 1990s. Compare this aerial photograph with the one above. Extensive gardens have been cultivated, yet much of the original façade remains. Since 1984 Scalford Hall has been run as a management training centre, catering for conferences and the requirements of industry and commerce. Emphasis is placed on the well-being of their clients. Excellent food is served in the restaurant and during extensive training seminars buffet lunches are served in the large lounge. A speciality is Dickinson & Morris traditional Melton Mowbray pork pie served with Colman's mustard.

Carol Treloar, head chef, at the main
entrance of Scalford Hall with a tray of
Dickinson & Morris pork pies.

Tony Moore enjoying a salad made with Dickinson &
Morris Melton Mowbray pork pies complemented
with a pint of Ruddles ale and Colman's mustard, a
speciality of the Hall that is always included in their
cold buffets.

Liz Howitt on the patio eating her pork pie salad in delightful surroundings. The extensive gardens are
open to all organisations and individuals using the facilities. Wedding receptions at Scalford Hall, Scalford
Road, Melton Mowbray, are a speciality of the establishment.

ACKNOWLEDGEMENTS

In the autumn of 1995 it was suggested to the author by a number of people including the Prime Minister John Major that a book should be written on the history of the pork pie trade in Melton Mowbray. The author took up the challenge. This book has been compiled with the help of many people. When the author approached the Chairman of Samworth Brothers Limited, David C. Samworth CBE DL, he gave him his full support; without his generosity this book would not have been produced in the way that it is now presented. Special mention must be made of Stephen Hallam's help. Stephen is the Managing Director of Dickinson & Morris (part of Samworth Brothers group of companies), the only surviving Melton Mowbray pork pie manufacturer in the town. He provided the author with help in his researches and made available the resources of this famous pork pie producer. Also to Alan McWhirr and the Leicestershire Archaeological and Historical Society for providing the photograph of Walker's shop. The author thanks the following people, who have provided information, illustrations and historic photographs:

Squire de Lisle, Ray Young, Jan Oldfield, Jean Morris, Rigby Graham, Roy Watts, Walter Simpson, Joan Morris, Leonard Harker, Helen Mapletoft, Prue Anderson, Alan Tucker, Barbara Bailey, Lilian Bailey, Guy Gilman, Jean Musto, Dennis Kirk, John Burgin, Sarah Burgin, Bob Heygate, Laurie Pearson, Jill Austin, Walter Skerritt, Warwick Forryan, Don Smart, Phil Andrew, Ian Hartland, Jane O'Donnell, Davina Bates, Pippa Morris, Paul Brown, Nick Rooney, Jim Graham, Rosemary Smith, Matthew Brown, Peggy Woods, Bet Woods, Janice Musson, Dawn Sanson, Lynne Bysouth-Kent, Jane Barnard, Neil Finn, Edna Wood, Mike Jackson and Christine Mason of the Bodleian Library.

Thanks must also be recorded to the staff of the many bakeries and butchers' shops that the author visited while conducting his researches during autumn 1996 and spring 1997. This has also resulted in some splendid traditional hand-raised pork pies being served on the author's dinner table, to his family; once again he records his thanks for their support and help. Angela Hickman prepared the author's hand-written manuscript for the publisher's use, for which grateful thanks are recorded. Some of the photographs printed here are covered by separate copyright, and in these cases permission has been granted to reproduce them! However, should this not be the case concerning some photographs, Trevor Hickman offers his sincere apologies for reproducing them without permission and will make an acknowledgement in future editions.

The author (left) gains 'hands-on' experience in the production of a traditional hand-crafted Melton Mowbray pork pie at Dickinson & Morris's bakery on Nottingham Street, Melton Mowbray.

LIST OF PLACES & FEATURES

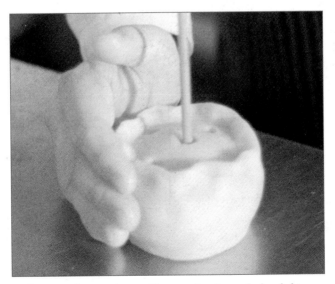

Piercing the lid of a Melton Mowbray pork pie with a wooden skewer before baking.